# CROSS STITCH
# KITCHEN
# PROJECTS

# CROSS STITCH KITCHEN PROJECTS

## JANET GRANGER

Guild of Master Craftsman Publications Ltd

First published 1997 by
Guild of Master Craftsman Publications Ltd,
166 High Street, Lewes,
East Sussex, BN7 1XU

© Janet Granger  1997

ISBN 1 86108 063 8

The Guild would like to thank Morris & Murray Designs
for their generosity in allowing us to use their showrooms
for the photography for this book

Photographs by Dennis Bunn

Line drawings by John Yates

Charts produced by Peter Rhodes

Designed by Teresa Dearlove

Typefaces: Akzidenz Grotesk and Lithos

Originated and printed in Singapore under the supervision of MRM Graphics

**TO MY HUSBAND CHRIS**
Thank you for giving me the security
I need to take risks.

**ACKNOWLEDGEMENTS**
I would especially like to thank the people who
did an excellent job of stitching my designs
for the photographs used in this book.
They are: Pat Gee, Ruth Green,
Judy Manktelow, Victoria Marshall and
Christine White. Thanks are due to
all the staff at GMC Publications, especially
Lindy Dunlop. Thanks also to
Framecraft Miniatures Ltd,
for the use of their products in
several of the projects.

# CONTENTS

## A NOTE ON MEASUREMENTS

Some materials used in cross stitch are only sold in metric units while others are commonly sold in imperial measures, and although the fabrics are now sold in metres, they are still always described in terms of 'holes per inch' (hpi). For ease of use, the measure in which a particular material is most commonly bought and sold is the one given first, with a metric or imperial equivalent (as relevant) given in brackets. The equivalent measures are not exact: in each case they have been rounded up or down to give a useful guide to those not familiar with the more common system of measurement.

# INTRODUCTION

**COUNTED CROSS STITCH** is a wonderful hobby: it is totally absorbing, needing concentration, yet relaxing at the same time. In the past few years it has become hugely popular, and there are many possible reasons for this, one being that it takes such a short time to learn the basic skills, but a lifetime to execute all those designs you've been stockpiling for 'when you've got time'! Even in today's busy world, it is good to relax at the end of the day with your stitching. How many times have you tried to limit yourself by saying 'I'll just finish the blue' or 'I'll just finish this flower', and before you know it, you've threaded the needle again and you're off!

It can be difficult to explain the sense of satisfaction gained from cross stitch to those who have yet to discover this hobby. If you are new to cross stitch, then read the next few pages on getting started before picking a design which interests you – more experienced stitchers can just dive in. I firmly believe that, even if you are a complete beginner, you need to be interested in what you are stitching. Don't necessarily attempt the smallest design first, and work methodically through them all. Feel free to take a motif from, say, a shelf edging, and put it on a coaster. Change the thread colours, or the fabric, to suit your chosen colour scheme. These designs should be seen as a starting point for your own creativity, so don't be afraid to experiment. I hate the phrase 'the possibilities are endless', however, the possibilities are there; you just need to decide what adaptations to make to

my designs, in order to make them into your own. At the end of each project, I have listed some variations you might like to try. These are just ideas to get you thinking. If you have ideas other than those I have suggested, that's great.

If you choose to work the designs exactly as they are presented in this book, that's fine too! Anyone who tells you that working other people's designs is 'cheating', probably wouldn't know one end of a needle from the other. From my experience, meeting all sorts of stitchers (some of whom have stitched the samples for the photographs in this book), there are thousands of people who quietly do exquisite needlework, and who never get any recognition for it. They play down their expertise when they shouldn't. We should stand up and be counted!

When I was thinking of ideas for this book, I decided on kitchen projects because as a theme it offers so much scope. Egg cosies, traycloths, teapot stands – all can be enhanced by cross stitch. There are 30 designs presented, ranging from tiny motifs for place-cards, which could be worked in an evening, to more ambitious projects such as the 'Tree of Life' tray, which could take several weeks. Each design has been given a difficulty rating as follows:

⊠ Easy

⊠ ⊠ Intermediate

⊠ ⊠ ⊠ Experience needed

**Poppy Placemat
and Coaster.**

Many of the projects would make beautiful gifts for friends and family. It is always lovely to receive a gift that has been made specially. So often these days, even 'craft' gifts are bought, not made at home. Time spent making a present shows that you care, and this book gives you plenty of ideas to choose from. Alternatively, treat yourself, and begin to transform your own kitchen into a showcase for your stitching talent.

Some projects have been designed to be matching sets, for example, the Poppy Placemat and Coaster set on page 41.

In addition to the difficulty rating, each project includes a colour key (listing Anchor, DMC and Madeira equivalents), materials list, method and ideas for variations and finishing.

Above all, enjoy it!

# MATERIALS AND EQUIPMENT

**CROSS STITCH DOES** not require a great outlay to get started. All you need to stitch a simple design is fabric, threads, needles and a good pair of scissors. Of course, there are many gadgets and accessories that can be bought (some of them very helpful), but these are not essential and can be gathered 'along the way'.

## FABRIC

### BLOCKWEAVE AND AIDA

Most of the projects in this book are worked on Aida fabric. This is a cotton, blockweave fabric used for counted cross stitch. The warp and weft threads are woven in blocks, so that a regular pattern of holes is left – this makes it simple to use, and easier on the eye than evenweave. Blockweave is available in various counts or holes per inch (hpi). If there are 14 holes to 1in (2.5cm) of the fabric, it is known as 14 count. If you completely covered this fabric with cross stitches, you would stitch 14 x 14, or 196, crosses on a square inch (5½ x 5½, or 30 per square centimetre).

I have found that 14 count is the most versatile, as you can achieve a lot of detail in the designs, without damaging your eyes. I have also used 18 count for a few of the projects – if you are new to cross stitch, you may find this finer count a bit more tricky to work with.

In addition to being available in several counts, Aida can be bought in a huge range of colours, from the palest of pastels to Christmas red, as well as the more usual white and cream – you can even get Aida with a lurex thread woven into it, which gives a lovely shimmering effect to special projects.

Many items for the home can be bought in specialist needlework shops with Aida panels in them, so you don't even need to be an expert seamstress. I have used several of these ready-made items (such as the Cook's Apron on page 28) to give you an idea of what can be done with these. Hand towels are another kitchen item that can be bought, in many different shades, with a matching Aida strip for you to embellish.

Aida band is a narrow strip of fabric, decoratively bound at the edges, which can be used very effectively for shelf edgings or cakebands. If you want to add cross stitch to household items and you cannot obtain specially designed 'cross-stitchable' ones, you could stitch your design onto a piece of Aida band – which is available up to 4in (10cm) wide – and slip-stitch it in place afterwards.

### VINYLWEAVE

Vinylweave is a 'fabric' which looks similar to Aida, but which, as the name suggests, is in fact vinyl. It is moulded in one piece, so has the advantage that it can be cut without fraying. This is useful for projects where the edge of the fabric will be visible (and is good, therefore, for items that fit in clear plastic mounts, such as napkin rings or coasters), but where turning a hem under, it would make the item bulky. A further disadvantage is that it is usually only available in white or cream, though you can stitch the whole of the background to achieve a different colour. Remember that a finished piece of stitching on this fabric cannot be ironed, as the 'fabric' would melt.

It is a bit more tricky to stitch on than blockweave fabrics as it is prone to split if the thread is tugged too hard, and once split it cannot be repaired.

## EVENWEAVE

Evenweave fabrics, such as linen, can also be used for cross stitch. The crosses are usually worked over two threads, so you would buy a 28 count linen (that is, 28 threads per inch) in place of a 14 count Aida, to achieve a finished piece of the same size. Because you count the threads of the fabric rather than single blocks, evenweave is slightly more difficult for counting than blockweave. Linen is quite expensive, but the quality can be felt in the fabric. For projects such as the Festive Wreath Tablecloth (see page 98), where good draping qualities enhance the finished look of the item, it is ideal. It is slightly more difficult to work with than Aida, as your counting needs to be carefully done (especially if placing odd stitches here and there on a pattern), but don't let that put you off – it's only counting, after all!

## AVAILABILITY

Most fabrics are available by the metre (or by the yard) from specialist needlework suppliers. However, very often you will only need a small piece in order to work a particular project. Most retailers realize this, and in the last few years it has become much more common for fabrics to be sold in 'pieces', say 20 x 20in (50 x 50cm) or even smaller. Some shops sell packs of cut pieces of mixed colours, such as 'pastel collections', or 'Christmas brights', often at a better price than if you were to buy each colour individually. Keep an eye on the classified advertisements in needlework magazines – mail order specialists are often the best places to get a really good deal.

## CONVERTING HOLES PER INCH TO METRIC

Although fabric is usually sold by the metre now, its count is still described in terms of holes per inch. If you are completely metric-thinking (well done – I wish I could do it!), it may seem meaningless to have a label on the fabric reading '14hpi'. As a rough guide, here are the popular counts of fabric, with their nearest metric equivalent:

11 squares per inch = 43 squares per 10cm
14 squares per inch = 55 squares per 10cm
16 squares per inch = 63 squares per 10cm
18 squares per inch = 71 squares per 10cm
22 squares per inch = 87 squares per 10cm

# THREADS

## STRANDED EMBROIDERY COTTONS

The projects in this book have all been worked using stranded embroidery cottons, or 'silks', plus a little metallic thread here and there. Stranded cotton is readily available. It comes in skeins – usually 8m (8yd 2ft) long – and consists of six strands loosely twisted together. Most cross stitch is worked using two strands in the needle, with backstitch worked using one. When using more than one strand, your stitches will lie flatter if you separate the strands completely and then recombine them before threading your needle. This stops the thread from twisting up on itself while you work.

## ALTERNATIVES

There are a number of other embroidery cottons that can be used, including flower threads, soft embroidery cottons, and space-dyed threads. Flower threads are very finely spun. They are good for projects worked on 18 count fabric, as you need only use a single thickness of thread to achieve sufficient coverage. Soft embroidery cotton is woollier, and more loosely spun than stranded cotton, so is good for projects worked on the lower count fabrics.

Space-dyed threads can be obtained from specialist manufacturers. The variegated shading of these skeins is sometimes so beautiful they seem almost too lovely to use. In practice they are often difficult to use success-fully as it is easy to get carried away with them. Restraint is needed so that you do not swamp your project with variegated colours. Using them in a narrow border, or just the leaves in a project, is probably enough to elevate the design to something really special.

I have used Balger blending filament and Anchor lamé thread when a metallic look is called for. These need just a bit more care than ordinary stranded cotton (see Starting and Finishing Threads, page 9).

The only disadvantage of using alternatives to the stranded cotton I have suggested, is that some of the other ranges have a limited selection of colours, and are only available by mail order. Once the cost of shade cards and postage is added on, they can work out quite expensive.

### WEAR AND TEAR

The threads of cross stitch fabrics can be quite rough, especially with evenweaves, and can wear through threads when they are continually rubbing against it. To prevent excessive wear on each length, it is best to use a piece no longer than 45cm (15in). This is a good size as the thread will remain in good condition right down to its end, but each length is not so short that you are forever re-threading your needle. Using the correct size needle for the particular fabric can also lessen wearing: a needle of the correct size will 'open up' the hole in the fabric sufficiently to cut down on unnecessary wear.

## NEEDLES

For cross stitch you need a tapestry needle. These have a large eye and a blunt tip. For most counts of fabric, a size 24 needle is best, but for finer work (22 count or finer), a size 26 is necessary. Ordinary sewing needles are far too sharp to use on fabric such as Aida – they would split the threads of the fabric. If you are working a design with a number of colours, it is a good idea to keep a needle threaded with each shade – this saves you a lot of time re-threading one needle. Needles do become dirty through contact with the skin, so remember to clean them occasionally. To do this, use a pincushion filled with an abrasive such as emery powder. Don't use the same needle forever – treat yourself to a shiny new one every once in a while.

## SCISSORS

You will need two pairs of scissors: a large pair of dressmaking scissors for cutting fabric, and a small pair of pointed embroidery scissors for cutting threads. It is a golden rule never to use your embroidery scissors to cut anything but your threads, but it is a very difficult rule to stick to! When stitching, it is a good idea to put your embroidery scissors on a ribbon loop and hang them around your neck. That way, they should be where you can find them when they are needed, and not down the back of the chair.

## FRAMES

I am a great believer in using a frame. By keeping your fabric taut, a frame can enhance the look of the finished item in a way no other embroidery 'accessory' can – it shouldn't be thought of as an extra. Several types of frame are available, from cheap and cheerful flexi-hoops to dedicated enthusiasts' floor-standing frames. If you are new to cross stitch, the variety available can be quite daunting, especially as the larger frames are quite expensive as well. The thought of perhaps wasting your money on something that you may use once and then leave to gather dust is a real consideration, but the staff in most specialist needlework shops are very willing to give honest advice as to which frame would be most suitable for the type of project and ability of the stitcher. For the larger floor-standing or seat frames, you might even be able to try 'sitting comfortably' at one before buying. Stitching shows and exhibitions are a good place to go for a 'practical advice and trying-out session'. (They are also good at extracting more money from you than you intended to spend – but that's just my experience!)

### HOOP FRAMES

Small projects can be worked using a hoop frame. This consists of two rings, one of which fits snugly inside the other. The fabric is placed over the inner ring, the outer ring is placed over the fabric and, once the fabric has been gently pulled even and taut all round, tightened with a screw fitting. A hoop frame is generally better for small projects as with a large project, any surrounding fabric tends to get in the way, although you can try rolling up the excess fabric and pinning it close to the frame. A further difficulty is that with a large design, you need to remove the fabric from the hoop and re-position it several times in order to complete the design. You also need to be careful not to trap any stitches between the two rings, or they will become permanently misshapen, thus spoiling your work. The creases formed by the rings can be difficult to iron out on some fabrics, but to minimize this you can wrap the inner hoop with bias binding to cushion the fabric a little.

Flexi-hoops consist, again, of two concentric shapes, and work in the same way as ordinary embroidery hoops. They have a fairly soft plastic outer ring with a hanging loop attached. Once the stitching is complete, instead of removing the stitching from it, the hoop is left in place to become the permanent 'picture frame' for the piece. Although known universally as hoops, they are available in several shapes – including ovals and squares – and many colours. It is possible, therefore, to co-ordinate the frame with your design very successfully using a flexi-hoop.

## ROTATING FRAMES
Rotating frames consist of two dowels with webbing attached, which slot into two side bars. The fabric is

then tacked squarely onto the strips of webbing, and the dowels rolled outwards until the fabric is held taut. Wing nuts hold the dowels in place and prevent the fabric from becoming slack. For extra tautness, you can lace the fabric up the sides, around the side bars, every inch or so (see Fig 1), although for projects which are not too big and will not be on the frame for any length of time, this is not essential.

Variations on this type of frame include those where pairs of 'bars' of different lengths are bought: four sides can be slotted together quickly to make rectangular frames of different dimensions. Some frames incorporate side bars which are collapsible, so that you can assemble your frame quickly for working on, then fold down the sides (to remove the tension on the fabric) for storage. This makes the frame more portable – an important consideration.

## FRAME STANDS AND ATTACHMENTS
There is nothing worse than the excruciating back pain that comes from stitching in an uncomfortable position. Having decided to invest in a frame, it really is a sensible idea to go for it and buy some kind of stand as well, so that you can really relax and enjoy your stitching. Both hoops and rotating frames can be used in conjunction with different types of stands. You

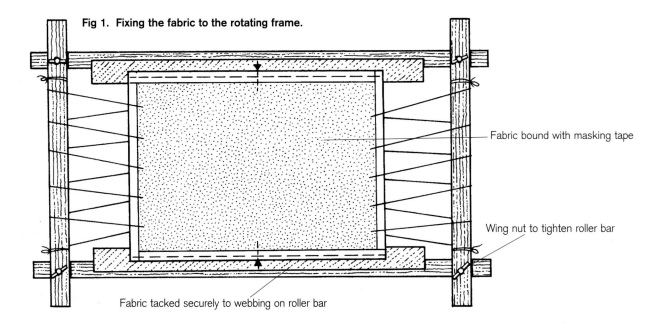

Fig 1. Fixing the fabric to the rotating frame.

Fabric bound with masking tape

Wing nut to tighten roller bar

Fabric tacked securely to webbing on roller bar

will need to decide where you will be doing most of your stitching, as the type of chair you sit in whilst sewing will have a big impact on the kind of frame stand which is suitable for you. Do you carry your stitching with you when travelling, for instance? Do the frame and stand need to be quickly collapsible, and light? When at home, if you stitch sitting in a comfortable chair with arms on it, you might find it difficult to manoeuvre some types of frame close enough for you to work. If you sit at a table, or have a table to one side, you will obviously have more choice of surfaces on which to place or clamp a frame stand.

If you intend working using a hoop, then a seat frame is a good investment. These have a shaped foot, which you tuck under your thigh to hold the stand steady, and an upright piece with a clamp, onto which you attach the hoop. They often have a quick-release mechanism at the clamp end, so that you can flip the hoop up easily to get access to the back of your work when tying off ends of thread.

Table frames and floor-standing frames are rotating frames which, as their names suggest, come attached either to short side supports, which stand on a table, or longer supports, which reach the floor. So that the frame can be angled to exactly the right position, most frame stands of this type have joints tightened by wing nuts, so your work can be tilted as much as you need. It is useful to have this flexibility when working on a large project, as you need to sit in a different position when making stitches on the fabric at the top of your frame, from when stitching those at the bottom.

## OPTIONAL EXTRAS

Like most hobbies, there is an immense range of extras which you can buy. It's great to walk into a well-stocked needlework shop and see row upon row of gadgets and accessories. So what if you don't necessarily need them? They are all part of the fun of cross stitching! Accessories can vary in price from the really cheap, such as floss bobbins, to one-off, carefully planned purchases such as angle-poise lamps with daylight bulbs and built-in magnifiers.

A floss bobbin is a piece of card or plastic, usually about 1 x 1½in (2.5 x 4cm), onto which you wind thread

in order to keep it tidy and organized. They are usually shaped like the silhouette of a cotton reel. Once you start to use a skein, it can easily become tangled, so floss bobbins are a good way to store part-used skeins. A slit cut in the edge of the bobbin can be used to hold the loose end of thread, to stop it unravelling.

Daylight bulbs are a wonderful invention – they fit into existing lighting sockets, and can extend your available stitching hours far into the night! Ordinary tungsten lighting gives a light which is far too yellow, making it difficult to tell shades apart, especially pale ones. Daylight bulbs, however, have a blue coating on the bulb's surface which filters out the yellowness of the light, balancing it out and giving a clearer, more white light – just like daylight, in fact.

Magnifiers are also available on their own in several forms. For instance, one type can be worn on a loop which goes around your neck, resting on a base which you stand on your chest. It sounds weird, but it works really well!

A good accessory to have, and one which I wouldn't be without, is a metal chart stand. You place your chart on the stand and use magnetic strips to help you keep your place on the chart. Just using one vertical and one horizontal strip to guide your eye to roughly the right area can make it much less tiring to read a chart. You can also buy magnetic 'pointers' (shaped rather like a mouse) to point to an exact square on the chart. Another use for the magnetic strip is that you can 'park' several needles in it, alongside your chart, threaded with the various colours you will need. This is much better than keeping them stored up the side of your fabric.

When you have been stitching for a while, you will probably find that you have quite a collection of partly-used skeins, so a storage system for these is a good idea. Floss bobbins (mentioned above) are one way to store them, and there are boxes of various types available which will hold these. Plastic pockets with slots to hold skeins are also available, and these will fit into ring binders. Whichever way you decide to store your thread, it helps to have them labelled and tidily to hand, so that they don't become a tangled mess. When you need a particular shade number you will be much more likely to find it, and when you come to design your own cross stitch pieces, just seeing the gorgeous colours set out neatly before you is enough to fire your imagination.

# MADE-UP ITEMS

There are now many made-up items available which include cross stitch fabric in them, a number of which are suitable for these kitchen projects. Towels with Aida band inserts are available in several colours and sizes, usually 14 count. Butcher-style aprons are also available, with either an Aida panel insert across the chest or on the pocket.

For smaller projects, napkin rings, coasters and light switch covers can be bought, with snap-lock acrylic covers to hold your completed stitching securely. It is often worth visiting a good needlework stockist for this kind of item before deciding on the design you want to stitch, as the products available can be an inspiration in themselves.

All of these ready-made items look very professional once personalized with your stitching.

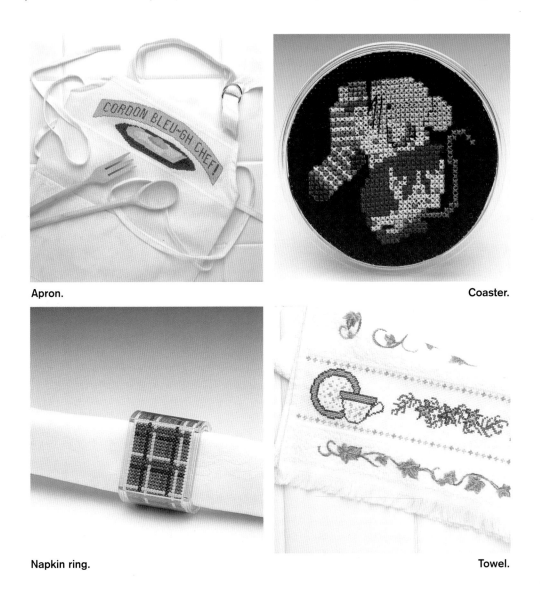

**Apron.**

**Coaster.**

**Napkin ring.**

**Towel.**

# BASIC TECHNIQUES

**ONE OF THE VIRTUES** of cross stitch embroidery is that it takes only a short while to learn how to do the stitch properly. You might be an absolute beginner, but within an evening you can master the stitch and be working on your first project. In this section I shall pass on some 'tricks of the trade' with regard to skills such as starting and finishing each length of thread neatly, as well as hints for working with metallic thread, which features in several of the designs.

## STARTING AND FINISHING THREADS

To begin with, you will obviously need to thread your needle. If you don't use the correct type (see Needles, page 5), this may be rather difficult! The eye of a size 24 or 26 needle is quite long and open, which is what you want – if you try to use an ordinary sewing (sharp) needle, the eye will be tiny, and you may well give up in frustration before you have even started stitching.

Cut a length of stranded cotton about 15in (45cm) long and, holding the thread between the thumb and forefinger of one hand, slowly, but firmly, pull one strand out of the six with the other hand. The remaining five strands will bunch up behind your thumb and forefinger, but will not become tangled if your movement is steady. When one thread has been fully removed, straighten out the remaining five strands and repeat the procedure. Thread your needle by gently twisting the ends of the two strands together

and pushing them through the eye of the needle. You might need to dampen the ends of the thread, but don't tell anyone that I told you to do this by putting them in your mouth (a very bad habit, and I'm sure no stitcher actually does it!). It is important to achieve a knot-free back to your work so that it will be neat and flat. To do this, knot one end of the thread, and work out where on the fabric you intend to start stitching. Then, take the needle from the front of the work to the back, about 1in (2.5cm) away from where you want to start stitching. This way, as you stitch you will catch the underlying thread in place. When you reach the knot, you can simply snip it off. Take care, when using dark thread on pale fabric, that there will be enough stitches covering the underlying thread to hide it sufficiently, otherwise, you might get a 'shadow' of thread showing through when you have finished.

When using metallic thread, such as Balger blending filament which is very thin, you can use the same method for starting, but to prevent the filament from slipping out, it is advisable to knot it to the needle (it will still go through the fabric). The knot at the other end, which anchors it to the fabric, will need to be big or it may slip through. Alternatively, you could simply hold the end of the thread with your left thumb while you make your first few stitches.

Whatever type of thread you are using, aim to finish stitching while you still have 3 or 4in (8–10cm) in the needle. It is very tempting to keep going just that little bit more, until there's so little left that you can barely turn the needle back on itself. This causes tight stitches and worn threads, and is unnecessary. End each length by running the needle under the backs of a few stitches, and snip off close to the fabric.

# CROSS STITCH

Following Fig 2, you can see that to make a cross stitch, you simply need to bring the needle up at 1, down at 2, up at 3 and down at 4. The procedure is the same, whether you are working on fine linen or a large-count Aida. All you need to remember is to stitch your cross over the same number of threads in each direction. On Aida, it will be over one block of threads. On evenweave,

**Fig 2. Working a cross stitch.**

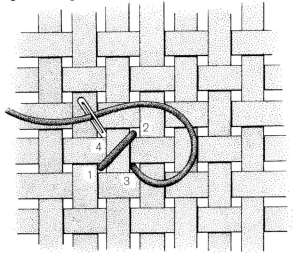

**Fig 3. Cross-stitching large areas of colour.**

it is usually two threads that you work over, although you can choose to count over one, two or even three threads, depending on the amount of detail you want, and the finished size and effect that you desire.

If you are working a row or large area in a single colour, it is easier to work a row of diagonal stitches in one direction, and then work back along the line making the top diagonal stitches to complete each cross (see Fig 3). This is a more economical way of stitching than completing one full cross stitch at a time before moving on – try both methods on a scrap of fabric to see. For the projects in this book, use two strands of cotton for working cross stitch, unless otherwise stated.

Always remember when working cross stitch, that the top diagonal stitches should all be pointing in the same direction over the whole design. It doesn't matter if it is top left to bottom right or the other way round (you will find you have a preference when you get started), but you must be consistent. If you are not, you will find that your work looks untidy, and that the light will catch stitches of the same colour in different ways, thus affecting the shading of your needlework.

## FRACTIONALS

There seems to be a fear of 'fractionals' in the cross-stitching world. Many kits proudly state 'No fractionals!' without mentioning what these weird and wonderful things are, perpetuating the myth that they are something horrific, to be avoided at all costs. To put the record straight, a fractional is simply a whole cross stitch that is worked in two stages, in two different colours, to give very fine definition to a design. It is not just that, say, the lower diagonal is worked in light blue and the top diagonal in dark blue, but, for instance, that the top left-hand quarter of the stitch is worked in light blue, and the remaining three-quarters in dark blue. This kind of 'fractional cross stitch' is much easier to achieve on evenweave fabric because, if you are working over two threads, it is easier to pass the needle through the fabric in the centre of a cross stitch, as there is a hole there already. On Aida, fractionals are much more difficult to execute neatly, as you have to split the threads of the closely woven blocks to force your needle through. Having explained all that, as almost all of the projects in this book have been specifically designed to be worked on Aida, I have decided that there will be no fractionals in this book!

## BACKSTITCH

Backstitch is used in many cross stitch designs – as outlining to add definition, or on designs which include lettering. I love combining lettering and embroidery, and,when used carefully, it is surprising how 'fluid' lines of backstitch can be. Whether it is representing curving tendrils on plant stems, or the explosion of a Christmas cracker, it is a very useful partner for cross stitch, and very simple to do. Following Fig 4, you bring the needle up at 1, down at 2, up at 3, down at 1 and so on, following the line on the chart. Even if the line appears to be a straight one, say, six squares long, you still work six individual short stitches rather than one long one. If the line on the chart passes diagonally across several squares, it is only possible to make a backstitch when the line passes exactly through an intersection, i.e. a hole, in the fabric.

**Fig 4. Working backstitch.**

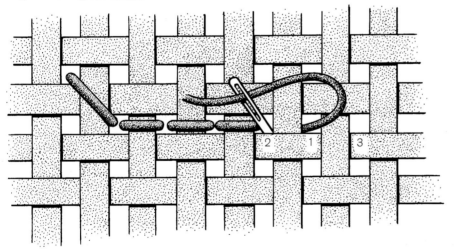

## STARTING YOUR WORK

Refer first of all to the 'Materials' section of the project you have chosen. This will tell you how much fabric you need. I find it best (almost always!) to start stitching from the centre of the design, so it helps to mark out your fabric with temporary centre lines, and to do the same with your chart, if it doesn't already have them marked. To find the centre of your fabric, fold it in half lightly both ways, and mark with pins where the two lines cross. In a shade of sewing cotton in contrast to that of your fabric, make tacking stitches vertically and horizontally across the fabric, following a line of holes exactly. These tacking stitches can be removed either gradually, as you stitch over them while you are adding the cross stitch, or all at once, when you have finished. Take care not to 'split the thread' of the tacking stitches as you work your crosses, or you may find the tacking thread difficult to remove afterwards.

The exception to the 'begin in the centre' rule is for long, thin fabric shapes, such as Aida band, where it is more sensible to start at one end, and work as many pattern repeats as necessary.

Having marked out the fabric, it is a good idea to bind the edges in some way to prevent unravelling, and also to stop your embroidery thread from catching on rough edges as you work. There are several alternative methods. You could turn a small hem and tack it in place temporarily, or if you have a sewing machine you could overlock the edge. Masking tape is a good and quick way to bind the fabric edge, but remember that it may leave a mark, or pull fabric threads when it is removed, so this method is best for projects where the fabric will be trimmed after the cross stitch has been worked. Fabric glues can be used very successfully to bind the edges of fabric. Just a light touch along the very edge is all you need (the bottles usually have a fine nozzle, so to apply only a tiny amount is easy).

If you intend to use a frame (which I recommend for all projects where it is practical to do so), the fabric is now ready to be mounted. Whichever type of frame you use make sure the fabric is held taut.

## STORING WORK IN PROGRESS

Only the tiniest of the designs can be worked in one stitching session, so adequate storage of work in progress is something you need to consider. If you have been using a hoop frame, it is best to remove the fabric from the hoop, because the marks from the rings can be difficult to iron out. The fabric should then be stored rolled – not folded – in a paper or cloth bag.

If you use a plastic bag to store 'work in progress' for any length of time, there is a risk that any dampness in the fabric could cause mould to grow. A paper bag will let any moisture escape. If you have mounted your fabric on a rotating frame, or something similar, it is neither necessary nor practical to remove it each time. Simply place a cotton cover of some kind (a pillowcase or tablecloth is ideal) over the whole frame to keep the dust off it.

Do not park your needle at the edge of the fabric as this may discolour or distort it. Invest in a pincushion or needle holder of some kind, as an incentive to be good!

Once your project is finished, if you are not ready to mount it or hem it immediately, the fabric should be stored rolled lightly in acid-free tissue, out of the light to prevent fading.

Acid-free tissue is what museums, artists and restorers use to store antique fabrics in and can be bought from artists' materials shops. If you store work in 'ordinary' tissue paper which has acid in it, the acid will eventually rot the fabric.

# TEN TIPS

**1** Always work in a good light. Apart from reducing the risk of inadvertently using the wrong shade of thread if you can't distinguish them easily, it isn't good for your eyes to work in shadow. Invest in a daylight bulb for a lamp which you can place near your work area (some spotlights can be clipped to your frame) if you stitch in the evenings.

**2** The top stitches of each cross should lie in the same direction across the whole of your design. This is easy to remember when working on small items because you can see the whole design in front of you, but for larger ones (such as the Festive Wreath Tablecloth on page 98), you will be working a motif, and then turning through 90° before working the motif again. It is important that the top stitches continue in the same direction as those on the first motif. If they vary, the stitches will catch the light differently, and cause the design to look darker or lighter in some places, ruining the desired effect. One way to make sure that all your stitches are worked in the same direction on large pieces, is to work a small piece of the design to get you started, then draw a large, double-headed arrow on a piece of paper to show the direction of your top stitches, and pin or tape this to the fabric. That way, as you turn your fabric to work further motifs, you will have an obvious reminder of the direction in which you should be working your stitches.

**3** Keep food and drink out of reach. Although it is tempting to have a cup of coffee to one side, and a packet of biscuits on the other while you stitch (I know I am guilty of this!), it increases the risk of messy spills and sticky fingers damaging your stitching. Eat first – then settle down to your needlework!

# FOR BETTER CROSS STITCH

**4** Keep fluffy things away from your stitching. This means pets, mohair jumpers, and so on. Apart from the fact that pets love pouncing on your threads (mohair jumpers are much more well-behaved), they are also likely to distract you from your counting, so mistakes are more likely to occur. The main reason, though, is that pet hairs and fluffy wool fibres from jumpers tend to get 'woven in' as you stitch. Once in, the hairs are almost impossible to remove and on some fabrics, they can be extremely noticeable – especially after you have framed your work under glass.

**5** Keep the back of your work knot-free. Whether the reverse of the fabric will be accessible or not, it is worth cultivating the habit of starting each thread length using the knot-free method explained on page 9. Your stitching will lie flatter once finished, and look much more professional.

**6** Always wash your hands before a stitching session, as pale fabrics and threads can easily become soiled. Also, do not use hand cream just before stitching, as the oil and perfumes contained in it could mark the fabric.

**7** Make sure you are comfortable while you stitch. Invest in some accessories to help you – a book rest is a good idea, so that you don't have to strain to see your chart. A cushion in the small of your back can help your posture, so that you don't become twisted up and aching after a few minutes. If you use a frame, move it around every half hour or so, so that your body shifts to a new position, to prevent getting stiff. Even if you want to stitch for hours (and who doesn't, given half a chance?), get up every hour or so and have a stretch, or a walk around, just to loosen up a little.

**8** Keep the threads for your current project tidy and organized, so that you can find the colour you want quickly and easily. You can make your own 'thread palettes' on which to store the threads you are using, very cheaply and easily. Cut a piece of cardboard from a cereal packet, and use a hole punch to make holes along one edge every inch or so. Cut the thread into 30in (76cm) lengths, loop each bundle of threads of one colour through one of the holes, and write the shade number alongside it. It should then be easy to remove one strand from the palette.

**9** Make sure that you are using the correct size needle for the fabric and thread. For most of the projects in this book, 14 or 18 count fabric is used, so a size 24 tapestry needle is suitable The 'Materials Needed' section for each project lists what size needle you need. As a guide, the needle should go through the fabric easily, with no need for tugging. It should make a big enough hole in the fabric to get the thickness of strands in the needle through, and no more. It should not be so thin that it falls through on its own.

**10** Use a frame! I will keep pushing this idea. Whatever sort you feel comfortable using will do. Even if you stitch whilst travelling, there are suitable frames you can use. A frame will ensure that your stitches lie evenly because the tension will be better. In addition, using a frame will often leave you with both hands free, so you can stitch quicker because you can rest one hand above and one hand below the fabric. It may also eliminate or reduce the amount of blocking or ironing that you need to do once the project is completed, as the fabric will be held flatter, more squarely, and more taut in the frame.

# USING AND ADAPTING THE DESIGNS

**THE CHARTS IN THIS BOOK** are all printed in colour for ease of use. They should, however, be taken only as a rough guide to how the finished project will look. To make them simple to work from, contrasts between similar shades have been exaggerated. Please refer to the colour photo of each completed project for a better idea of the real shades used.

## USING THE CHARTS

Each chart has arrows marking the centre lines. These are the centre lines of the design area, which is not always the centre of your fabric. For instance, the Dried Flowers Shopping List Board on page 25 is deliberately stitched off-centre to allow space for the notepad to be fixed alongside it.

One square on the chart always stands for one cross stitch on the fabric. Unless otherwise stated, use two strands for all cross stitch, and one for backstitch. The backstitch is marked by a heavy solid line on the charts, and should be worked after all the cross stitch has been completed, otherwise it tends to become 'swallowed up' by the cross stitches.

A colour key for each project lists the colours used, and how much you will need of each shade. The amounts given allow for wastage, and are rounded up to the nearest half metre (20in). It is worth checking over the design for those shades used in small amounts, then looking in your workbox to see if you have either a part-skein of the correct

colour, or even a similar one that would do as a replacement. It all helps to keep the cost down! The amount of thread used is based on the project being worked on the count of fabric recommended. If you choose to work the design on a different count of fabric (for instance, 14 instead of 18), your crosses will be a different size to the sample shown and you will therefore use a different amount of thread. All the projects in this book were worked using Anchor stranded cotton. DMC and Madeira equivalents are given, but please be aware that the shades listed are approximations only and may give a slightly different result.

Where a chart has been split over two or three pages, a four-row overlap has been printed on each side of the chart. This repeated strip is indicated by a line extending beyond the edges of the chart. Take care to stitch these rows only once.

## ADAPTING THE DESIGNS

These designs are for you to use how **you** want – adapt them as much as you like, or use them as a basis for your own embroidery design ideas. Each project has a section headed 'Variations', in which I have mentioned any ideas that sprang to mind as I designed them. Many people shy away from altering patterns to suit their own needs, but it really is very simple. Even small changes can make all the difference – and what you end up with is then unique.

## COLOUR SCHEMES

The simplest way to adapt a design is to alter the colours. If your kitchen is, say, pink and white, and you want to make the 'Stencilled' Tea Cosy on page 20, it is easy to work the design as given, and simply substitute a deep pink for the roses, and perhaps a dark red for the vase. Also, stitching the design on white Aida instead of cream will give you an item that will co-ordinate beautifully with the rest of your kitchen, without much scary redesigning at all.

Sometimes, altering the fabric colour alone is enough to change the look of a design. You can test this out by collecting together the threads you intend to use for a particular project, and then laying them on different colour fabrics to see the different effects. You could do this in the shop, or at home, using your own remnants.

## ISOLATED MOTIFS

Another way to adapt the designs is to pick out a small part of a larger design (such as a rose from the Festive Wreath Tablecloth on page 98), and work it as a single motif on other items. In this particular case, matching napkins would be a good idea. Isolated motifs often look very different when repeated several times to make borders, and a solid line or two of cross stitches above and below the pattern repeats, using one of the main colours from the motif, unites the whole thing to make it a design in its own right.

## DIFFERENT FABRIC COUNTS

Designs can look vastly different when worked on a different count of fabric. A design worked on, say, 14 count fabric, can look bold and stark, whereas the same design worked on a much finer 22 count linen can look dainty. Designs on finer counts often benefit from being worked in paler colours, because your cross stitch will look more dense if less of the background fabric is left showing around each stitch. Remember also that if you change the fabric to a finer one, you may need to use fewer strands of thread in your needle. Obviously, changing to a coarser fabric will mean that you need more strands. If you are unsure of what looks right, practise on a scrap of the fabric that you intend to use before starting on the real thing.

## CALCULATING THE FINISHED SIZE

If you alter the fabric count from that suggested, you will need to calculate the new size of your finished piece. To do this, you first need to know the maximum dimensions of the design, in stitches. You then divide these figures by the count of fabric you intend to use, to give the dimensions in inches. As an example, take a motif which measures 54 x 90 stitches. On 18 count fabric, your motif would be 3 x 5in (54 ÷ 18 = 3 and 90 ÷ 18 = 5).

If you prefer to work in metric measurements, work out the calculations as before, then multiply each of your final figures by 2.54 to give the motif's dimensions in centimetres. For example, the metric equivalents of a motif measuring 3 x 5in would be 7.6 x 12.7cm (3 x 2.54 = 7.6 and 5 x 2.54 = 12.7). This explanation always sounds a lot more complicated than it really is. If you are still unsure, work through the examples with a calculator and a ruler in front of you and, hopefully, it will become clearer!

# ONE

# 'STENCILLED' TEA COSY

When stencils are used on walls and furniture, it is usually to liven up plain, painted surfaces. With a stencilled design, shape is everything. It is like a silhouette. If a design is too fussy, the basic outline is lost, and all you are left with is a mass of blobs. Stylization is therefore important when designing stencils – it is the effect, rather than a 3-D representation, that you want. Here, full-blown roses have been simplified to six or seven petals each, yet they are still instantly recognizable.

**Design size**
7½ x 7in (19 x 18cm) on 14 count
**Stitch count**
104 x 96
**Materials**
Cream, 14 count Aida, 15 x 26in (38 x 60cm)
Cotton backing fabric, 15 x 26in (38 x 60cm)
2oz wadding, 15 x 26in (38 x 60cm)
Medium weight piping cord, 1m (1yd)
Bias binding, rust-coloured, 1m (1yd)
Threads as listed in the colour key
Size 24 tapestry needle

## WORKING THE DESIGN

Usually, stitching is started in the centre of the fabric, but for this design, make sure you leave at least 3in (7.5cm) of blank fabric below the bottom of the rose bowl to enable you to make up the teacosy. It will save you lots of counting if you outline the main area of the bowl first, then just 'colour it in' with dark claret (remembering to leave the 'holes' of the stencil pattern lower down the bowl). Stitch the roses themselves, then fill the spaces between them with the small leaves and stems. Stitch the two dark leaves last.

## FINISHING

Make a paper template following Fig 5. Centre the template on your stitching, leaving 3in (7cm) of clear fabric under the motif, and cut out. Use the template

again to cut one piece from plain Aida, two pieces from lining fabric and two from wadding. A ½in (1cm) seam allowance is included. Bind the piping cord within the bias binding. To make up the front, place the stitching face down, place a piece of wadding and a piece of lining fabric on top, and tack through all three layers. Repeat for the back, using the piece cut from plain Aida. Now place the front section (with stitching uppermost) on a flat surface, and tack the piping cord around the curved edge, with raw edges facing outwards. Next, place the back section on top of the front section, with the right sides together, and stitch around the curved edge with a sewing machine, leaving the bottom edge open. Finally, turn right side out and neaten the bottom by turning in and slip-stitching the edges together.

## VARIATIONS

If you want to make your design more like the painting technique of sponging, you could work each area of colour using variegated thread (see the Blue-and-white Shelf Edging on page 68 for an illustration of the effect this type of thread can have). To give the right shading effect, work each motif from the same side across the whole motif. Work each cross completely before going on to the next (i.e. don't do a row of diagonals and then cross them on the return journey). This way, the gentle shading of the thread will have the maximum impact. Alternatively, you could 'colour in' the design, and use a different colour for each rose, to match your kitchen tiles, for instance.

**Fig 5. Tea cosy template (25% actual size).**

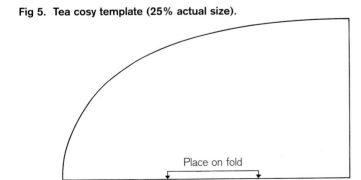

Place on fold

## Colour key

| | | Anchor | DMC | Madeira | Strands for cross stitch | Strands for backstitch | Amount |
|---|---|---|---|---|---|---|---|
| ■ | Dark claret | 360 | 898 | 2005 | 2 | – | 6m (6yd 1½ft) |
| | Golden yellow | 362 | 437 | 2012 | 2 | – | 7m (7yd 2ft) |
| ■ | Dark olive green | 846 | 3051 | 1507 | 2 | – | 2m (2yd 6in) |
| | Sage green | 859 | 522 | 1509 | 2 | – | 2.5m (2yd 2ft) |

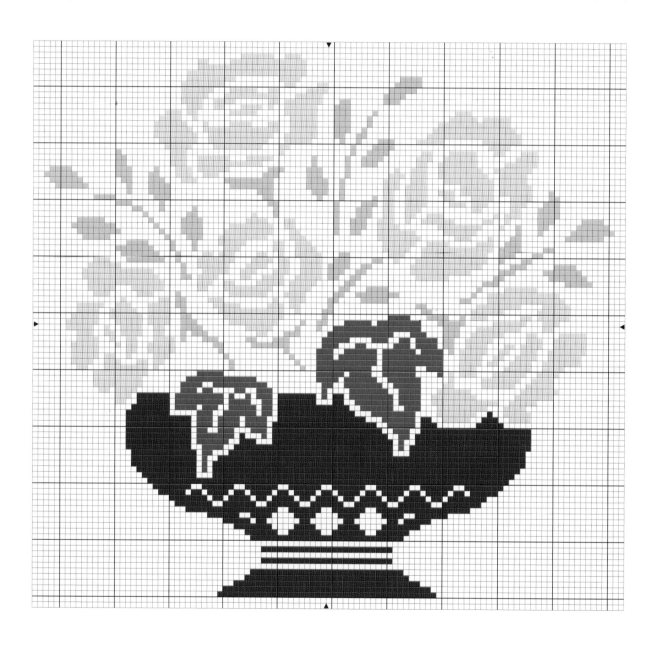

# TARTAN
# NAPKIN RING

For a beginner, this project is ideal, as it is quick and easy to do, has few colours and no complicated shading. Tartan has become a popular fabric design at Christmas, but can be used at any time of the year to give a more formal look to your dinner table.

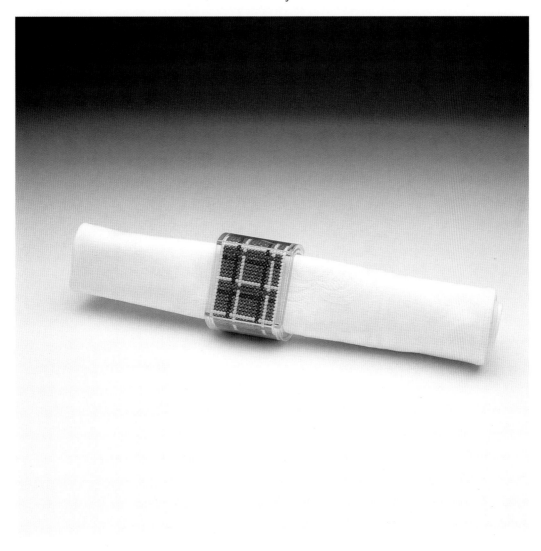

**Design size**
1½ x 5¾in (4 x 14.5cm) on 14 count
**Stitch count**
20 x 80
**Materials**
Clear plastic napkin ring, with cream, 14 count
Vinylweave insert, 1¼ x 5¾in (3 x 14.5cm)
Threads as listed in the colour key
Size 24 needle

## WORKING THE DESIGN

Start in the centre of the fabric, and work the stripes. Take care to get your 'under' and 'over' stripes correct!

When all the stripes are finished, fill in the background completely with the dark jade green, working up to the edges of the fabric as far as possible.

## FINISHING

Very carefully trim the vinylweave to within one square of your stitching, so that very little plain fabric is left showing, then wrap the fabric around the inner plastic ring, with the join underneath. Slide the outer ring over it, snapping it shut to hold the fabric in place securely.

## VARIATIONS

This design was worked on vinylweave and mounted in a bought napkin ring, but you could just as easily stitch it on Aida band and sew the strip into a circle afterwards for a softer ring. It would also be easy to change the colour scheme for this design.

**Colour key**

| | | Anchor | DMC | Madeira | Strands for cross stitch | Strands for backstitch | Amount |
|---|---|---|---|---|---|---|---|
| | Cranberry | 59 | 326 | 0603 | 2 | – | 1.5m (1yd 2ft) |
| | Very dark red | 72 | 814 | 0601 | 2 | – | 1.5m (1yd 2ft) |
| | Dark jade green | 212 | 561 | 1313 | 2 | – | 4m (4yd 1ft) |
| | Sand | 288 | 445 | 0103 | 2 | – | 1.5m (1yd 2ft) |

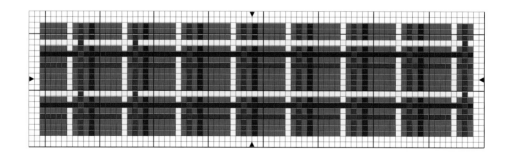

# DRIED FLOWER SHOPPING LIST BOARD

Dried flower arrangements always look pretty in a kitchen, but after a while they tend to lose their colour and become irreversibly dusty. Why not create your own version of a dried flower decoration in cross stitch, and display it alongside your shopping list pad? This project is based on a decorated brass spoon which I bought as a souvenir in Austria. The bowl of the spoon is very shallow, and pierced like a skimmer, which I have represented with dots of dark brown. Above that, a ribbon bow and silk cord hold the stems of the roses, ivy and fir fronds.

**Design size**
3¼ x 8¼ (8 x 21cm) on 14 count
**Stitch count**
46 x 115
**Materials**
Cream, 14 count Aida, 16 x 14in (40 x 35cm)
Shopping list pad, spiral bound,
2 x 7in (5 x 18cm)
Drawing pins x 4
Plywood 10 x 10in (25 x 25cm)
Threads as listed in the colour key
Size 24 tapestry needle

## WORKING THE DESIGN

The cross stitch needs to be placed off-centre to allow space for the notepad, so find the centre of the fabric, then measure 2½in (6.5cm) to the left to find the exact centre of the spoon motif before starting to stitch. Work the rosebuds first, and the pine cone, before working the surrounding greenery. Next, work the

ribbon bow and silk cord bow in shades of pink and red, then work the spoon itself. When all the cross stitch is complete, work the backstitch outlining to give definition. Remember to work the veins of the ivy leaves in backstitch as well.

## FINISHING

Mount the stitching on the plywood as if you were going to frame it (see Mounting and Framing, page 129). Make sure that there is a blank margin of 1in (2.5cm) from the top and bottom edge, and 1½in (4cm) on the left-hand side. In the space to the right of the spoon, position the notepad centrally between the top and bottom of the wood, and use the drawing pins, pushed through the backing card of the pad to hold it securely to the wood. Securing the pad in this way will enable you to replace it easily when necessary.

## VARIATIONS

The design could be worked on its own (without the notepad) and framed as a narrow picture. To give a more 3-D effect, work the design as given and attach extra ribbon, bows and cord, in shades to match your kitchen.

### Colour key

| | | Anchor | DMC | Madeira | Strands for cross stitch | Strands for backstitch | Amount |
|---|---|---|---|---|---|---|---|
| | Pale rose | 48 | 3713 | 0607 | 2 | – | 0.5m (1½ft) |
| | Medium rose | 50 | 957 | 0613 | 2 | – | 1m (1yd) |
| | Very dark red | 72 | 814 | 0601 | 2 | 1 | 1m (1yd) |
| | Deep rose | 76 | 3687 | 0604 | 2 | – | 1.5m (1½ft) |
| | Very dark green | 218 | 319 | 1405 | 2 | 1 | 1m (1yd) |
| | Yellow green | 264 | 3348 | 1604 | 2 | – | 1m (1yd) |
| | Medium green | 268 | 937 | 1504 | 2 | – | 1.5m (1yd 2ft) |
| | Light yellow | 300 | 745 | 0111 | 2 | – | 2.5m (2yd 2ft) |
| | Gold | 891 | 676 | 2208 | 2 | – | 1.5m (1yd 2ft) |
| | Copper | 898 | 611 | 2112 | 2 | 1 | 0.5m (1½ft) |
| | Dark brown | 905 | 3021 | 1904 | 2 | – | 0.5m (1½ft) |
| | Light Christmas red | 969 | 223 | 0809 | 2 | – | 1m (1yd) |
| | Christmas red | 972 | 3803 | 0603 | 2 | 1 | 2m (2yd 6in) |

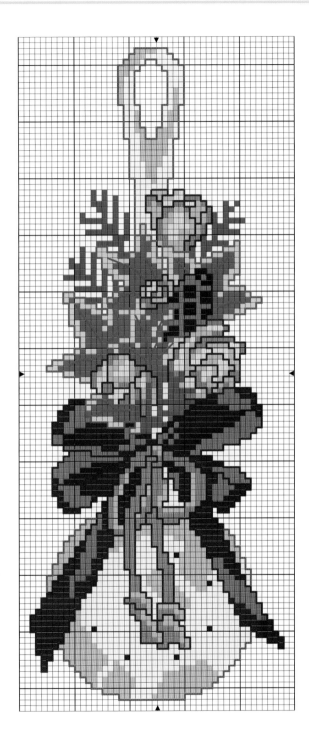

# COOK'S APRON

Not everyone is interested in cooking. If you know someone whose *pièce de résistance* is egg on toast, perhaps they would appreciate an apron acknowledging their skill? This apron is a shop-bought one, but if you wanted to, you could make your own apron and appliqué the Aida on afterwards.

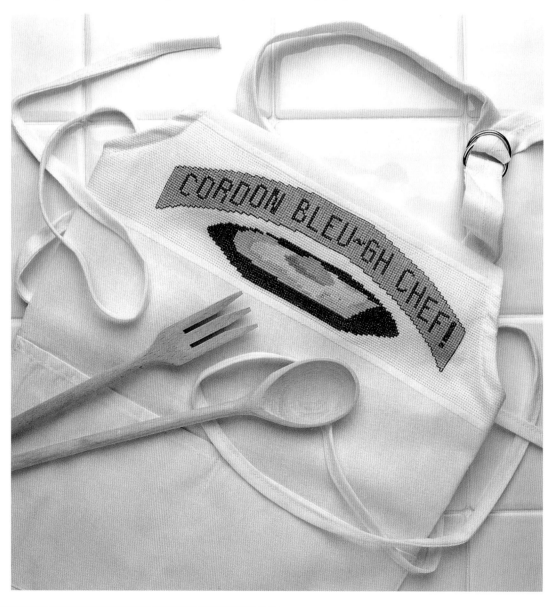

**Design size**
10 x 3½in (25.5 x 9cm) on 14 count
**Stitch count**
140 x 47
**Materials**
Ready-made apron in cream fabric, with 14 count
Aida panel insert
Threads as listed in the colour key
Size 24 needle

# WORKING THE DESIGN

Find the centre of the Aida panel, and start your stitching from here, working the 'egg on toast' motif first. The lettering panel will be easier to do if you stitch the letters first, from the centre outwards in each direction. After this, work the outermost line of pale canvas green cross stitches in the background: it is then simply a case of 'colouring in'. When all the cross stitch is complete, work the backstitch outline of the lettering panel.

# VARIATIONS

If the person you are stitching the apron for has a particular recipe that is always a disaster, you could try substituting a cross stitch representation of it for the egg on toast. Try to make it recognizable! Alternatively, you could just stitch their name on a smaller version of the lettering panel. Plan it on graph paper first, and shorten the ends of the banner as necessary.

**Colour key**

|  |  | Anchor | DMC | Madeira | Strands for cross stitch | Strands for backstitch | Amount |
|---|---|---|---|---|---|---|---|
|  | Pale canvas green | 206 | 966 | 1209 | 2 | – | 9m (9yd 2ft 6in) |
|  | Canvas green | 246 | 986 | 1313 | 2 | 1 | 4m (4yd 1ft) |
|  | Dark green | 269 | 936 | 1507 | 2 | – | 1m (1yd) |
|  | Autumn gold | 297 | 444 | 0108 | 2 | – | 0.5m (1½ft) |
|  | Light yellow | 300 | 745 | 0111 | 2 | – | 1.5m (1yd 2ft) |
|  | Burnt orange | 304 | 741 | 0202 | 2 | – | 0.5m (1½ft) |
|  | Beige | 311 | 3827 | 2301 | 2 | – | 1.5m (1yd 2ft) |
|  | Coffee brown | 351 | 400 | 2305 | 2 | – | 1m (1yd) |
|  | Dark claret | 360 | 902 | 0601 | 2 | – | 0.5m (1½ft) |
|  | Very pale grey | 397 | 762 | 1804 | 2 | – | 0.5m (1½ft) |

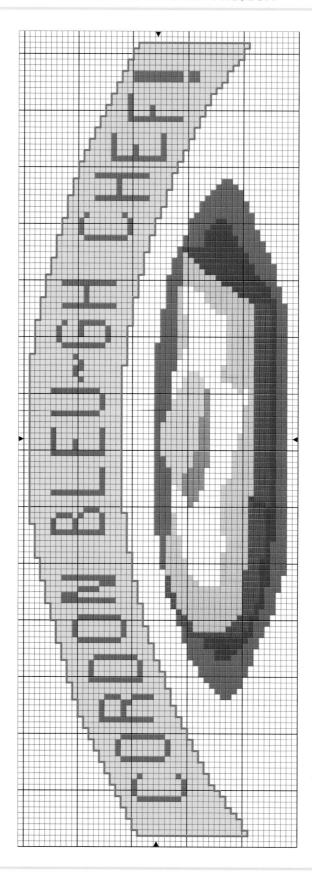

# CUP AND SAUCER TEA TOWEL

I really like designing for functional items like this tea towel. What better way to display your stitching skills than on something you can actually use as well? There are many towel sizes and all-over designs available now – this ivy leaf pattern is on quite a small towel, making it ideal for use as a tea towel. The cup and saucer motif could easily be moved outwards, slightly away from the centre flowers, to fill a wider band. Most towels such as this one have an Aida band insert of 14 count fabric, but they are sometimes 16 count, or even 18 count, so check first before buying.

**Design size**
13 x 2¾in (33 x 7cm) on 14 count
**Stitch count**
181 x 39
**Materials**
Cotton towel with ivy leaf pattern, 14 x 22in
(36 x 56cm), with white, 14 count Aida
band insert of 14 x 3in (36 x 7.5cm)
Threads as listed in the colour key
Size 24 tapestry needle

## WORKING THE DESIGN

Carefully measure to the centre point of the Aida band insert, and begin your stitching from here, working the larkspur flowers and fern fronds. Next, work the dark mauve outline and mauve bands of the cups and saucers, before stitching the flower and leaf details of the china pattern. Finally, work the top and bottom borders in shades of pink and lilac, as indicated on the chart.

## VARIATIONS

If you have an ordinary towel on which you would like to work this design, it is possible to buy Aida band up to 4in (10cm) wide. Work the design on the band as detailed above, then slip-stitch in place on the towel, turning the short sides under ½in (1cm) to neaten them. The larkspur centre motif could also be repeated on narrower Aida band, and used as a co-ordinating shelf edging. Or you could adapt the pattern on the cups and saucers to match your own china. If you feel this is a bit ambitious, simply alter the main colours of the design to the colour scheme of your kitchen for an easy way to achieve a co-ordinated look.

**Colour key**

| | | Anchor | DMC | Madeira | Strands for cross stitch | Strands for backstitch | Amount |
|---|---|---|---|---|---|---|---|
| | Hot pink | 86 | 3608 | 0709 | 2 | – | 1m (1yd) |
| | Dusty pink | 95 | 211 | 0801 | 2 | – | 1m (1yd) |
| | Mauve | 104 | 209 | 0803 | 2 | – | 2.5m (2yd 2ft) |
| | Palest lilac | 108 | 210 | 0802 | 2 | – | 1m (1yd) |
| | Dark mauve | 112 | 333 | 0713 | 2 | – | 3m (3yd 1ft) |
| | Light olive green | 214 | 368 | 1310 | 2 | – | 0.5m (1½ft) |
| | Dark sea green | 245 | 986 | 1214 | 2 | – | 1m (1yd) |
| | Gold | 891 | 676 | 2208 | 2 | – | 0.5m (1½ft) |

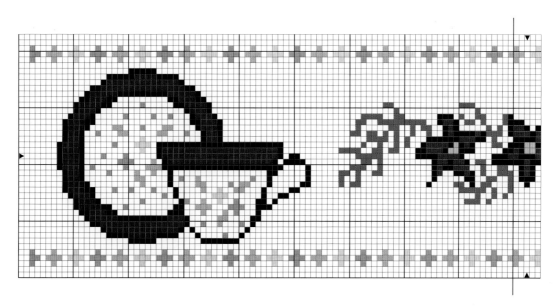

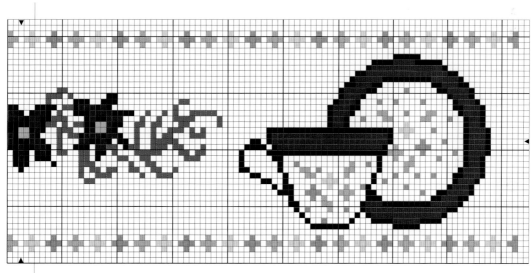

# TWO

# 'TREE OF LIFE' BREAKFAST TRAY

Tree of life designs were very popular in the sixteenth and seventeenth centuries, often depicted on bed-hangings, curtains and wall-hangings in the houses of the rich. They were usually worked in crewel wools, using a wide variety of stitches. Here, I have adapted a crewel embroidery version into cross stitch, using geometric pattern repeats to suggest couched and laid threads, and close shades worked in rows to suggest long- and short-stitch shading. The colours of this design are deliberately muted, to give the impression of age.

**Design size**
9 x 6½in (23 x 16.5cm) on 14 count
**Stitch count**
124 x 93
**Materials**
Silver grey, 14 count Aida, 13 x 16in (33 x 60cm)
Wooden tray, 12 x 9in (30 x 23cm), with
oval aperture of 7 x 10in (18 x 25.5cm)
Threads as listed in the colour key
Size 24 needle

## WORKING THE DESIGN

Find the centre of the fabric and, counting out a little to the right of this before starting to stitch, work the trunk of the tree and main branches in shades of brown, then work the three hills at the base. After that, it is simply a case of picking a flower or leaf motif, and working it completely before moving on to the next. You may find it easiest if, with each motif, you work the outline before working the detail. Once all the cross stitch is completed, work the backstitch tendrils, outlines and veining on the leaves in the appropriate colour.

## FINISHING

Wash and press your stitching if necessary (see Finishing, page 128). Trim the fabric to 1in (2.5cm) larger all round than the mounting board of the tray. Lace the fabric to the mounting board in the same way that you would a picture to be framed (see Mounting and Framing, page 129). Alternatively, secure the fabric to the board using pieces of masking tape to hold it taut. Insert the baseboard, mounted needlework and protective glass into the tray base, holding all three in place with the brass fixing screws supplied.

**Colour key**

| | | Anchor | DMC | Madeira | Strands for cross stitch | Strands for backstitch | Amount |
|---|---|---|---|---|---|---|---|
| | Pale green | 213 | 369 | 1309 | 2 | – | 1.5m (1yd 2ft) |
| | Green | 215 | 320 | 1311 | 2 | – | 2.5m (2yd 2ft) |
| | Deep green | 217 | 367 | 1312 | 2 | 1 | 2m (2yd 6in) |
| | Fawn | 830 | 822 | 1907 | 2 | – | 1m (1yd) |
| | Medium brown | 832 | 640 | 1911 | 2 | 1 | 1.5m (1yd 2ft) |
| | Pale violet | 870 | 3042 | 0807 | 2 | – | 1m (1yd) |
| | Lilac | 871 | 3041 | 0802 | 2 | – | 1m (1yd) |
| | Deep violet | 873 | 3740 | 0803 | 2 | – | 1m (1yd) |
| | Branch brown | 889 | 869 | 2107 | 2 | 1 | 1.5m (1yd 2ft) |
| | Pale peachy pink | 892 | 3774 | 0501 | 2 | – | 1.5m (1yd 2ft) |
| | Dusk pink | 894 | 224 | 0813 | 2 | 1 | 1.5m (1yd 2ft) |
| | Claret | 896 | 3721 | 0811 | 2 | – | 2m (2yd 6in) |
| | Light blue | 920 | 932 | 1710 | 2 | – | 1m (1yd) |
| | Blue | 921 | 931 | 1711 | 2 | – | 1.5m (1yd 2ft) |
| | Dark blue | 922 | 930 | 1712 | 2 | – | 2.5m (2yd 2ft) |

## VARIATIONS

If you like the idea of stitching a tree of life design, but don't have a tray base, how about adapting the tree to be much taller and thinner, and making a bell-pull from it instead? All you need to do is draw a wavy line on some graph paper to the chosen length of your bell-pull. Not too many kinks are needed – you want to leave wide gaps for the placement of the leaves and flowers. Make the line wide at the base and narrow at the top, then take the motifs from the tray design and position them on your 'beanstalk'. It will help at this planning stage if you just cut out extra pieces of graph paper to the maximum stitch dimensions of each motif, so that you can move each piece around until you are happy with the composition. Once you are satisfied, stick the 'motif guide shapes' in place, add a few tendrils to fill any gaps, and start stitching from your chart, referring to the original one for the details. Bell-pull ends, in brass or wood, are widely available from needlework shops to add the finishing touch.

# POPPY PLACEMAT
# AND COASTER SET

Poppies are such unruly plants, but are always a welcome sight.
Although there are many cultivated varieties available now, I have chosen
the wild poppy, in traditional red, to decorate this placemat and coaster set.
The poppy is a plant that refuses to be tamed, so the placemat design
features blooms facing in all directions – some full-blown,
some just opening. I have stitched these designs on Rustico fabric,
which adds to the country feel.

⊠ ⊠

**Design size**
Placemat: 5¾ x 5¼in (14.5 x 13cm)
Coaster: 2¼ x 2¼in (5.5 x 5.5cm)
**Stitch count**
Placemat: 79 x 73
Coaster: 32 x 31
**Materials**
Placemat: Rustico (beige flecked), 14 count Aida,
17 x 13in (43 x 33cm)
Coaster: Rustico (beige flecked), 14 count Aida,
5 x 5in (13 x 13cm)
Threads as listed in the colour key
Size 24 needle

# WORKING THE DESIGNS

### PLACEMAT

The design is to fit into the bottom left-hand corner of the mat, so measure up 3in (7.5cm) from the bottom edge of the fabric and 3in (7.5cm) in from the left-hand edge. This point is the bottom left corner of the design – start stitching from here. Work the clump of leaves in various shades of green, then the stems growing out from them. Work the petals next, taking care to distinguish the red tones, as the shading is very gradual. Lastly, work the black centres of the poppies. When all the cross stitch is completed, work the backstitch details.

### COASTER

Start in the centre of the fabric and work the design elements in the same order as for the placemat: leaf, stem, then flower. Work the backstitch last.

# FINISHING

### PLACEMAT

To fringe Aida or evenweave, decide the exact size you want the fabric to be before allowing for fringing, and stitch along this line with a sewing machine, using a thread to match the fabric colour. Trim the fabric outside this line to ¾in (2cm) all round, following a thread of the fabric exactly, then gently tease out the unwanted fabric threads up to the stitched line, leaving an even fringe on all four sides (see Fig 6).

**Fig 6. Fringing fabric.**

Pull out long fabric threads
Trim fabric to same depth all around
Sew a line to prevent unravelling
Completed fringe

### COASTER

This can be finished in the same way as the Christmas Mouse Coaster (see page 85).

# VARIATIONS

The poppy placemat motif could be rotated through 180° and repeated in the top right-hand corner of the mat, or even worked in the four corners of a matching tablecloth. The poppy coaster design could be worked on a higher count fabric (such as 18 or even 22), and a lighter fabric colour – perhaps cream – as a ceramic pot lid motif. Ceramic pots are available in several colours, and down to really tiny sizes – just right to keep your rings in, while you work in the kitchen.

## Colour key for placemat

| | | Anchor | DMC | Madeira | Strands for cross stitch | Strands for backstitch | Amount |
|---|---|---|---|---|---|---|---|
| | Dark coral | 13 | 817 | 0211 | 2 | – | 1.5m (1yd 2ft) |
| | Deep pink | 35 | 891 | 0410 | 2 | – | 1m (1yd) |
| | Strawberry red | 46 | 666 | 0210 | 2 | – | 2m (2yd 6in) |
| | Cranberry | 59 | 326 | 0603 | 2 | – | 1m (1yd) |
| | Dark gold | 306 | 783 | 0114 | 2 | – | 0.5m (1½ft) |
| | Coffee brown | 351 | 400 | 2304 | 2 | – | 0.5m (1½ft) |
| | Black | 403 | 310 | Black | 2 | – | 0.5m (1½ft) |
| | Oregano green | 843 | 3012 | 1607 | 2 | – | 2m (2yd 6in) |
| | Pale forest green | 860 | 3363 | 1513 | 2 | – | 1m (1yd) |
| | Dark fern green | 862 | 935 | 1514 | 2 | – | 0.5m (1½ft) |
| | Gold | 891 | 676 | 2208 | 2 | – | 0.5m (1½ft) |
| | Hazelnut brown | 906 | 829 | 2113 | 2 | – | 1m (1yd) |

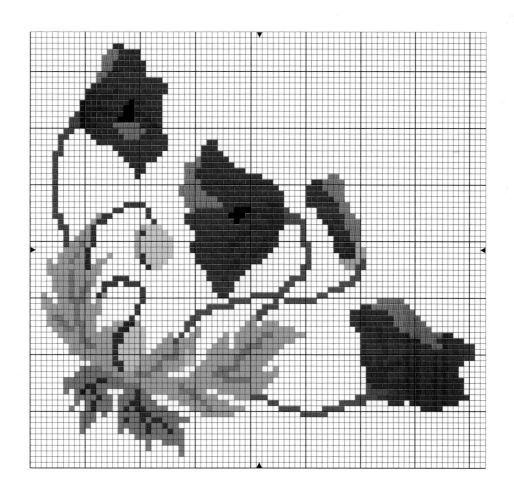

## Colour key for coaster

| | | Anchor | DMC | Madeira | Strands for cross stitch | Strands for backstitch | Amount |
|---|---|---|---|---|---|---|---|
| | Dark coral | 13 | 817 | 0211 | 2 | – | 0.5m (1½ft) |
| | Deep pink | 35 | 891 | 0410 | 2 | – | 0.5m (1½ft) |
| | Strawberry red | 46 | 666 | 0210 | 2 | – | 0.5m (1½ft) |
| | Cranberry | 59 | 326 | 0603 | 2 | – | 0.5m (1½ft) |
| | Black | 403 | 310 | Black | 2 | – | 0.5m (1½ft) |
| | Oregano green | 843 | 3012 | 1607 | 2 | – | 1.5m (1yd 2ft) |
| | Pale forest green | 860 | 3363 | 1513 | 2 | – | 0.5m (1½ft) |
| | Hazelnut brown | 906 | 829 | 2113 | 2 | – | 0.5m (1½ft) |

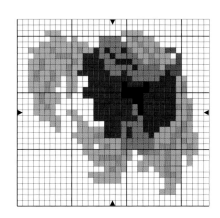

44

# 'HOME SWEET HOME' SAMPLER

A cosy kitchen cannot be considered complete without some kind of
country-style sampler on its walls. The heart of the home always seems
to be the kitchen, and this is the place people gravitate to at the end
of a tiring day. It is also where the best conversations take place!
Whether or not your home actually looks anything like the type
of building depicted in this sampler doesn't really matter –
it is the archetypal image of a comfortable home.

### Design size
5¾ x 3¾in (14.5 x 9.5cm) on 14 count
### Stitch count
81 x 53
### Materials
Rustico (beige flecked), 14 count Aida,
9 x 12in (23 x 30cm)
Oval wooden frame,
5 x 7in (13 x 18cm)
Threads as listed in the colour key
Size 24 needle

## WORKING THE DESIGN

Start in the centre of the fabric and stitch the door and windows of the house, then fill in the walls using ecru. Work the roof next, stitching the 'replaced tiles' in straw gold. Work outwards from the house on either side, stitching the flower, tree and cat. The lettering can then be worked, using the three shades of olive green, finishing off top and bottom with a row of hearts. Once all the cross stitch is completed, work the backstitch where indicated on the chart.

## FINISHING

Wash and press your work if necessary (see Finishing, page 128), then take the glass from the oval frame and centre it over your stitching. Draw around the glass with a pencil, then trim the fabric to just inside the pencil line. Place the glass and fabric in the frame, and fix the backing board in position, checking that the stitching is exactly square.

## VARIATIONS

To personalize this picture, you could add your initials and the date. To do this, either take out one or two of the motifs (such as the flowers, or some of the hearts) to give you enough space, or use a larger picture frame. You could even substitute a cross stitch version of your own home for the one I have used. Try to use the same palette of colours for any additions you make though, as too many shades in one design can look fussy and disjointed.

### Colour key

| | | Anchor | DMC | Madeira | Strands for cross stitch | Strands for backstitch | Amount |
|---|---|---|---|---|---|---|---|
| | Deep red | 20 | 815 | 0512 | 2 | – | 1m (1yd) |
| | Straw gold | 308 | 782 | 2211 | 2 | – | 0.5m (1½ft) |
| | Pastel olive green | 844 | 3012 | 1607 | 2 | – | 0.5m (1½ft) |
| | Medium olive green | 845 | 3011 | 1614 | 2 | – | 1m (1yd) |
| | Dark olive green | 846 | 3051 | 1507 | 2 | 1 | 2m (2yd 6in) |
| | Branch brown | 889 | 869 | 2107 | 2 | – | 0.5m (1½ft) |
| | Dark brown | 905 | 3021 | 1904 | 2 | 1 | 0.5m (1½ft) |
| | Ecru | 926 | Ecru | Ecru | 2 | – | 1m (1yd) |

# SUMMER FLOWERS DOOR FINGERPLATE

Fingerplates for doors are usually porcelain, decorated with painted designs or transfers. This fingerplate, however, is made of clear plastic, under which you can display these sprays of summer flowers, worked in bright shades. The design was inspired by German folk embroidery, which is usually worked in long and short stitch on linen, to a pre-printed outline on the fabric. The flowers are always very stylized, which adds to the naive quality.

**Design size**
2 x 9¾in (5 x 25cm) on 14 count
**Stitch count**
28 x 136
**Materials**
White, 14 count Aida, 6 x 14in (15 x 35cm)
Clear plastic door fingerplate,
2 x 10in (5 x 25.5cm)
Threads as listed in the colour key
Size 24 needle

# WORKING THE DESIGN

Start in the centre and stitch the large red and orange flower first, then the buds and leaves of the same plant. Moving up, stitch the flowers, then the buds and leaves of the top motif. Work the lower motif in the same way. When all the cross stitch is complete, go back over the whole design, working the stems in backstitch.

# FINISHING

Wash and press your work if necessary (see Finishing, page 128). Place the plastic fingerplate over the stitching and draw a pencil line around the edge. Place the card mount evenly within this pencilled line, and mark around the card. This will ensure that your design is centred properly. Cut just inside the inner line with very sharp scissors. Mount the fabric and backing card in the recess of the fingerplate, and secure in place with the backing card. Fix to the door using four screws.

# VARIATIONS

Any one of these motifs could be used in isolation on a number of kitchen items, and still look complete: the three motifs are each small enough to be used on herb bags or egg cosies. Another option would be to repeat the three sprays of flowers several times on a long piece of Aida band, and use it to add a decorative edging to curtains.

## Colour key

| | | Anchor | DMC | Madeira | Strands for cross stitch | Strands for backstitch | Amount |
|---|---|---|---|---|---|---|---|
| | Dark Christmas red | 44 | 347 | 0407 | 2 | – | 0.5m (1½ft) |
| | Strawberry red | 46 | 666 | 0210 | 2 | – | 1m (1yd) |
| | Medium pink | 73 | 604 | 0614 | 2 | – | 0.5m (1½ft) |
| | Deep rose | 76 | 3731 | 0610 | 2 | – | 0.5m (1½ft) |
| | Palest lilac | 108 | 211 | 0801 | 2 | – | 0.5m (1½ft) |
| | Wisteria | 111 | 208 | 0804 | 2 | – | 0.5m (1½ft) |
| | Lavender | 117 | 3747 | 0907 | 2 | – | 0.5m (1½ft) |
| | Darkish blue | 134 | 820 | 0904 | 2 | – | 0.5m (1½ft) |
| | Pale leaf green | 240 | 369 | 1209 | 2 | – | 1m (1yd) |
| | Yellow | 289 | 307 | 0104 | 2 | – | 0.5m (1½ft) |
| | Mango | 330 | 947 | 0205 | 2 | – | 0.5m (1½ft) |
| | Deep leaf green | 923 | 699 | 1303 | 2 | 1 | 1m (1yd) |
| | Iris | 978 | 322 | 1004 | 2 | – | 0.5m (1½ft) |

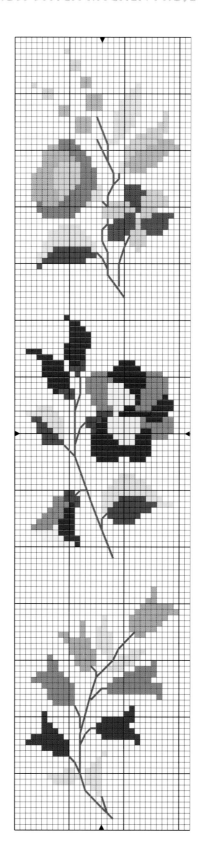

# LIGHT SWITCH PROTECTOR PLATE

The wallpaper or paint around light switches can easily become grubby, so clear plastic protector plates are a really good idea. Why not use this 'extra surface' as another area on which to stitch? This design uses a simple pattern of checks in shades of blue to give a French feel. The addition of the daisies, placed randomly around the edges, adds to the airy quality of this project.

**Design size**

5½ x 5½in (14 x 14cm) on 14 count

**Stitch count**

75 x 75

**Materials**

White, 14 count Aida, 8 x 8in (20 x 20cm)

Clear plastic light switch protector plate, 6 x 6in
(15 x 15cm), with aperture of 3 x 3in (7.5 x 7.5cm)

Iron-on interlining, 6 x 6in (15 x 15cm)

Threads as listed in the colour key

Size 24 tapestry needle

## WORKING THE DESIGN

As this design is, in effect, a border pattern, it is more sensible to start stitching in one corner than in the centre of the fabric. Therefore, measure 1in (2.5cm) in from the bottom edge and the left-hand edge of the fabric, and begin stitching from here. Stitch the daisies and blue check pattern in a sweep around the fabric – do not stitch the widely-spaced daisies first, in case you miscount;

unpicking is very disheartening! The backstitch can be done once all the cross stitch is complete.

## FINISHING

Wash and press your fabric if necessary (see Finishing, page 128), then iron a piece of interlining onto the back, about ½in (1cm) bigger all round than your stitching. With a sharp pair of scissors, cut away the excess fabric around the outside and inside of your needlework. The interlining will help to keep its shape. Place the trimmed fabric in the plastic plate, with the cardboard template (supplied with the plate) behind it. You may need to use a tiny piece of tape to hold the three layers together while you unscrew the light switch slightly and position them under the rim. Make sure that you turn off the electricity supply first. Screwing the light switch down tightly again will hold the plate securely.

## VARIATIONS

The blue checks can easily be changed to match the décor of your own kitchen. If you stick to using a dark shade where I have used one, and so on, the pattern will look very similar in tone when finished.

### Colour key

| | | Anchor | DMC | Madeira | Strands for cross stitch | Strands for backstitch | Amount |
|---|---|---|---|---|---|---|---|
| | White | 1 | Blanc | White | 2 | – | 2m (2yd 6in) |
| | Raspberry pink | 52 | 899 | 0413 | 2 | 1 | 0.5m (1½ft) |
| | Medium blue | 121 | 794 | 0906 | 2 | – | 4m (4yd 1ft) |
| | Deep purple blue | 123 | 791 | 0914 | 2 | – | 4m (4yd 1ft) |
| | Light cornflower blue | 159 | 827 | 1710 | 2 | – | 4m (4yd 1ft) |
| | Tangerine | 302 | 743 | 0114 | 2 | – | 0.5m (1½ft) |

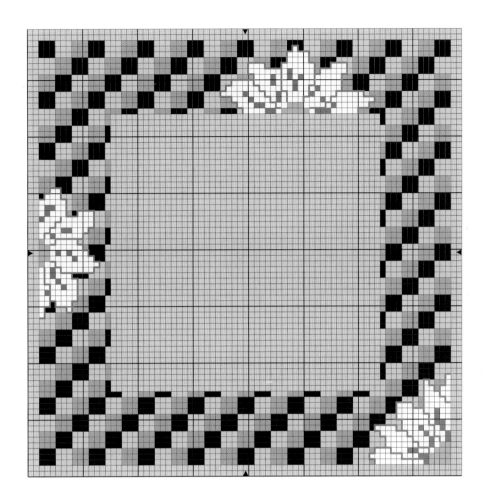

# THREE

DELFT TRAYCLOTH
HIS AND HERS EGG COSIES
HERB BAGS
BLUE-AND-WHITE
SHELF EDGING
SQUARE DELFT COASTER
POT HOLDER

# DELFT TRAYCLOTH

Delftware became hugely popular in England in the late-seventeenth century, so much so that English manufacturers copied the Dutch designs to the last detail, to cash in on the fashion. This traycloth design is taken from a tile made by a Liverpool factory in the mid-eighteenth century, and depicts a typical rustic scene. Related motifs taken from other eighteenth century delftware tiles have been set along each side of the main design, to create an ambitious project for those with some needlework experience.

**Design size**
15½ x 9¼in (40 x 23.5cm) on 14 count
**Stitch count**
218 x 128
**Materials**
White, 14 count Aida, 14 x 21in (36 x 54cm)
Threads as listed in the colour key
Size 24 tapestry needle

## WORKING THE DESIGN

Starting in the centre, work the buildings and trees, then continue with the harbour wall and two boats, and the border of the main picture panel, before stitching the sea. Obviously, as the sea colours are mixed at random, it is not vital to stitch the sea exactly as printed on the chart. You may prefer to work by eye, and place the stitches in rough 'bands' of colour, working in from the edges and using the darker shades first: this will achieve the same effect. Once the centre panel is complete, stitch the borders of the six small side panels before working the small motifs within them. When all the cross stitch is finished, go back over the design working the backstitch.

## FINISHING

To make up your traycloth, see Hemming, page 129.

## VARIATIONS

If you would like to work this design, but feel that the 'shimmering sea' effect is too difficult for you, you could adapt the chart and work the whole area of the sea in one strand of Anchor 130, in half cross stitch. This will give a delicate water effect, without the complicated counting! Make sure that your stitches lie in the same direction as the top diagonals of your whole cross stitches. The complete design could be used as a placemat rather than a traycloth, with one of the small side motifs worked again to make a square coaster to match.

## Colour key

| | | Anchor | DMC | Madeira | Strands for cross stitch | Strands for backstitch | Amount |
|---|---|---|---|---|---|---|---|
| | Navy blue | 127 | 823 | 1008 | 2 | 1 | 22m (24yd) |
| | Very pale blue | 128 | 3753 | 1001 | 2 | – | 4m (4yd 1ft) |
| | Baby blue | 130 | 809 | 0909 | 2 | – | 8.5m (9yd 1ft) |
| | Darkish blue | 134 | 820 | 0913 | 2 | 1 | 7m (7yd 2ft) |
| | Medium blue | 147 | 312 | 0911 | 2 | 1 | 10m (11yd) |

# HIS AND HERS EGG COSIES

This pair of egg cosies features Dutch children in traditional costume, complete with clogs. They make an attractive matching set, and, as they are small designs and use only three colours, will only take a few hours to complete.

⊠

**Design size**
1¾ x 3in (4.5 x 7.5cm) on 14 count
**Stitch count**
25 x 43 (maximum)
**Materials (for two cosies)**
Marine blue, 14 count Aida,
10 x 13in (25.5 x 33cm), cut into four pieces,
5 x 6½in (13 x 16.5cm) each
Narrow white ribbon for loops
Threads as listed in the colour key
Size 24 needle

## WORKING THE DESIGNS

Start in the centre of each chart, and work the hands first, then the clothing, then the head. When all the cross stitch is completed, work the backstitch outlining and facial details in dull marine blue.

## FINISHING

Make a paper template following Fig 7, and centre your stitching on it. Cut out the stitched fabric (the template includes ½in (1cm) seam allowances), and a plain piece for the back, to the same size. Fold a short piece of ribbon into a loop, and tack in place at the centre top of the stitched front piece, with the loop hanging downwards. Place the two halves of the cosy together, right sides in, and sew around the curved edge on a sewing machine. Clip around the curve every ¼in (6mm) up to the sewn line, and turn through to the right side. Turn the bottom edge up ¼in (6mm) and stitch a hem, or seal with a touch of fabric glue instead, to prevent unravelling.

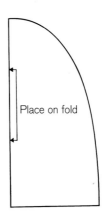

**Fig 7. Egg cosy template (50% actual size).**

Place on fold

## VARIATIONS

I have chosen to work these Dutch figures in the traditional blue and white, but it would be simple to 'colour in' the design, using any combination of colours you may have to hand. To match your egg cosies, you could work the motifs again on a napkin, or a traycloth. A row of alternating girls and boys would make an attractive border for a kitchen towel or apron hem, too.

| Colour key for both cosies | | Anchor | DMC | Madeira | Stands for cross stitch | Strands for backstitch | Amount |
|---|---|---|---|---|---|---|---|
| ⬜ | White | 1 | Blanc | White | 2 | – | 1m (1yd) |
| ⬛ | Dull marine blue | 150 | 823 | 1007 | 2 | 1 | 2.5m (2yd 2ft) |
| ▨ | Pale marine blue | 849 | 927 | 1708 | 2 | – | 2.5m (2yd 2ft) |

# HERB BAGS

Herbs are invaluable in the kitchen. Even if you have no garden in which to grow them, a hanging basket or even a terracotta pot by your back door will provide an adequate space for your own crop of freshly grown herbs to live happily until needed. Once the herbs have been dried, these bags are an ideal place to store them, and much prettier than glass jars! The set uses a limited range of colours to give a co-ordinated look to the bags. Lavender, a beautiful-smelling herb with many medicinal properties (it is wonderful for alleviating headache), is not often used in cooking. A good place to keep this bag, therefore, is in your tea towel drawer, so that each new tea towel will come out smelling of this heady herb.

⊠ ⊠
**Design size (each bag)**
2½ x 5½in (6.5 x 14cm) on 14 count
**Stitch count (for each)**
33 x 76
**Materials (for all three bags)**
Sky blue, 14 count Aida, 21 x 17in (54 x 43cm),
cut into six rectangles, 7 x 8in (18 x 21.5cm) each
Lace or anglais for trimming bags, 1.4m (1½yd)
Ribbon for tying bags, 1.4m (1½yd)
Threads as listed in the colour keys
Size 24 tapestry needle

## WORKING THE DESIGN

To leave enough space at the top of the fabric for the ribbon to be tied, start by stitching the rectangular border in shaded olive green thread. The rectangle should be centred right to left across the fabric, leaving a margin of only 1in (2.5cm) at the bottom, and about 2½in (7cm) at the top. Shaded thread is interesting to work with, and gives lovely effects, but has to be used with a little more forethought than plain threads. Make sure that when you finish each length, you start the next length with the same shade, so that the colours flow across the design. It makes using variegated threads a bit wasteful sometimes, but the effect is well worth it. Once the border rectangle has been worked, you can place your herb motif within it, working the cross stitch stems and leaves first, and then the flowers before working the backstitch details on the stems and leaves. Finally, stitch the name of the herb in the lower box, using one strand of dark olive green.

## FINISHING

Take your stitched piece, and a piece of plain Aida of the same colour and size, and sew the two together, right sides in, ½in (1cm) in from the sides and bottom (Fig 8). Leave the top open. Turn the bag right side out. Turn down the top edge of the bag to neaten it, and at the same time, tack the lace or anglais in place across the top. The lace or anglais can then be

securely attached either by sewing machine or by hand, using slip stitch, making sure that the Aida hem is caught in place. Finally, add a narrow ribbon to keep the bag's contents secure.

**Fig 8.**
**Making up a herb bag.**

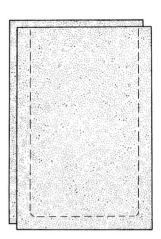

Front and back of herb bag, right sides facing, sewn together along three sides, as indicated by dotted lines

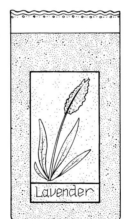

Lace trim sewn onto top edge

Herb bag turned right side out

Lavender

## VARIATIONS

These herb motifs would look totally different if stitched on a different colour fabric – so if blue doesn't suit your kitchen, choose another colour instead. As each design is of a uniform size, they could be worked on one piece of fabric to make a picture panel. You could even design a few more herb pictures, within the same size rectangular border, to make a larger picture or larger set of bags, specifically tailored to the herbs that you most often use. Cookery books are a good source of pictures for this, or art books featuring botanical prints.

## Colour key for lavender bag

| | | Anchor | DMC | Madeira | Strands for cross stitch | Strands for backstitch | Amount |
|---|---|---|---|---|---|---|---|
| | Shaded olive green | 216 | 320 | 1311 | 2 | – | 1m (1yd) |
| | Pale olive green | 266 | 470 | 1502 | 2 | – | 0.5m (1½ft) |
| | Medium green | 268 | 937 | 1504 | 2 | – | 0.5m (1½ft) |
| | Pale grey green | 842 | 3013 | 1605 | 2 | – | 0.5m (1½ft) |
| | Dark olive green | 846 | 3051 | 1507 | 2 | 1 | 0.5m (1½ft) |
| | Pale lilac | 869 | 3743 | 0807 | 2 | – | 0.5m (1½ft) |
| | Lilac | 871 | 3041 | 0806 | 2 | – | 0.5m (1½ft) |
| | Palest dusty pink | 893 | 761 | 0404 | 2 | – | 0.5m (1½ft) |
| | Dusk pink | 894 | 224 | 0813 | 2 | – | 0.5m (1½ft) |

## Colour key for marjoram bag

| | | Anchor | DMC | Madeira | Strands for cross stitch | Strands for backstitch | Amount |
|---|---|---|---|---|---|---|---|
| | Shaded olive green | 216 | 320 | 1311 | 2 | – | 1m (1yd) |
| | Pale olive green | 266 | 470 | 1502 | 2 | 1 | 1m (1yd) |
| | Medium green | 268 | 937 | 1504 | 2 | 1 | 1m (1yd) |
| | Pale grey green | 842 | 3013 | 1605 | 2 | 1 | 0.5m (1½ft) |
| | Dark olive green | 846 | 3051 | 1507 | 2 | 1 | 0.5m (1½ft) |
| | Pale lilac | 869 | 3743 | 0807 | 2 | – | 0.5m (1½ft) |
| | Lilac | 871 | 3041 | 0806 | 2 | – | 0.5m (1½ft) |
| | Palest dusty pink | 893 | 761 | 0404 | 2 | – | 0.5m (1½ft) |
| | Dusk pink | 894 | 224 | 0813 | 2 | – | 0.5m (1½ft) |

## Colour key for thyme bag

| | | Anchor | DMC | Madeira | Strands for cross stitch | Strands for backstitch | Amount |
|---|---|---|---|---|---|---|---|
| | Shaded olive green | 216 | 320 | 1311 | 2 | – | 1m (1yd) |
| | Pale olive green | 266 | 470 | 1502 | 2 | – | 0.5m (1½ft) |
| | Medium green | 268 | 937 | 1504 | 2 | – | 0.5m (1½ft) |
| | Dark beige | 378 | 407 | 1911 | 2 | – | 0.5m (1½ft) |
| | Pale grey green | 842 | 3013 | 1605 | 2 | – | 0.5m (1½ft) |
| | Dark olive green | 846 | 3051 | 1507 | 2 | 1 | 0.5m (1½ft) |
| | Pale lilac | 869 | 3743 | 0807 | 2 | – | 0.5m (1½ft) |
| | Palest dusty pink | 893 | 761 | 0404 | 2 | – | 0.5m (1½ft) |
| | Dusk pink | 894 | 224 | 0813 | 2 | – | 0.5m (1½ft) |

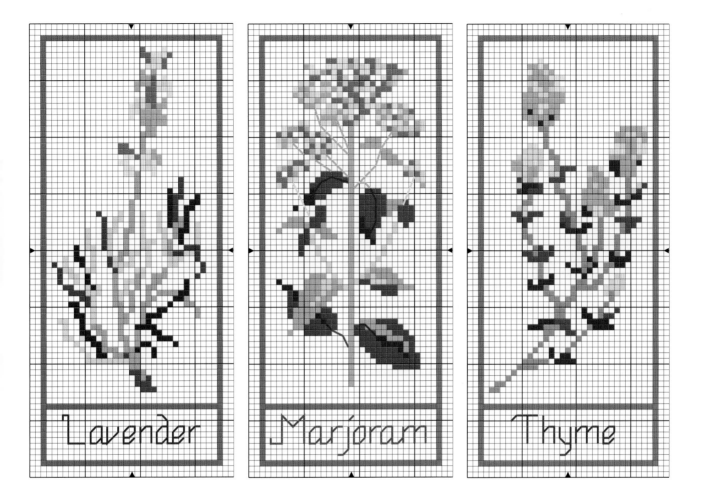

# BLUE-AND-WHITE SHELF EDGING

Shelf edgings are a quick and easy way to soften the look of a kitchen and give it a 'countrified' feel. If you don't own a dresser, you could still attach some Aida band to plain open shelves, taking the band around the sides of the shelves as well, to give a neater and more complete look. Aida band comes in many widths, and it is worth considering the scale of the furniture you intend to attach it to before you start to stitch. For instance, a massive Victorian, dark oak dresser would probably need a wider band than the 2in (5cm) one I have used here. If in doubt, try sticking strips of paper of different widths to your shelf fronts, to get an idea of what looks right.

**Design size**

1¾ x 36in (4.5 x 90cm)

**Stitch count**

23 high x length as necessary

**Materials (For 90cm (1yd) of shelf edging)**

White, 14 count Aida band, edged with pale blue,
2in (5cm)

Threads as listed in the colour key

Size 24 tapestry needle

## WORKING THE DESIGN

Measure your shelf, and use a piece of Aida band the total length of your shelf plus 2in (5cm) for turnings. Starting from one end, stitch the central wavy line of the pattern the full length of the band, using two strands of variegated thread, and making sure that the shades of blue 'flow' when you finish one length of thread and start another. Once this line is done, you can work the stylized flowers, from right to left across the whole flower, using royal blue. Work the tendrils last, using one strand of the shaded thread.

## FINISHING

Fix the band temporarily to your shelf with masking tape, and check that the pattern is balanced. Mark the total finished length of the shelf edging with a couple of pins, then take the band off the shelf and trim the ends of the band to within 1in (2.5cm) of each pin. Turn the excess fabric under and under again, and slip stitch in place. Attach the shelf edging to the shelf, using either drawing pins (paint the tops with white modellers' enamel paint to disguise them), or narrow strips of double-sided tape.

## VARIATIONS

If you prefer not to use variegated thread, but still want to use shades of a single colour to work the design, you could stitch the flowers using a pale shade for the central petal, a medium shade for the next two and a deep shade for the outermost petals. Aida band is so adaptable, it can be added to lots of other kitchen items, such as tea towels, traycloth edges or even kitchen aprons. Work the cross stitch as before, and slip stitch the finished band in place on all four sides, turning the two short sides under first in order to neaten them.

| Colour key | | Anchor | DMC | Madeira | Strands for cross stitch | Strands for backstitch | Amount |
|---|---|---|---|---|---|---|---|
| | Royal blue | 133 | 797 | 0913 | 2 | – | 8.5m (9yd 1ft) |
| | Shaded blues | 1210 | 995 | 1102 | 2 | 1 | 4.5m (4yd 3ft) |

# SQUARE DELFT COASTER

This dainty design only uses three colours, and is suitable for complete beginners. It is so small that it can be successfully completed in an evening. The shades of thread used match the Delft Traycloth design on page 58, so you could probably work this design using the part-skeins left over from the larger project.

**Design size**
2½ x 2½in (6.4 x 6.4cm) on 14 count
**Stitch count**
35 x 35
**Materials**
White, 14 count Aida, 5 x 5in (13 x 13cm)
Clear acrylic square coaster, 3¼ x 3¼in (8 x 8cm)
Threads as listed in the colour key
Size 24 tapestry needle

## WORKING THE DESIGN

Start in the centre of the design, and stitch the petals of the flower. Next, stitch the leaves in two shades of blue. Count out carefully to each corner and work each motif. When all the cross stitch is complete, work the backstitch lines.

## FINISHING

Trim the fabric until it just fits into the coaster, then iron it on the reverse side, on a padded board. Separate the two halves of the coaster, place the fabric between the two layers and snap shut. You may wish to place a piece of card, cut to the same size as your stitching, in the coaster first, to cover the back of the fabric and give a neater appearance.

## VARIATIONS

This design could be 'coloured in', using any part-skeins that you happen to have left in your workbox, to make a colourful set of square coasters, all different. The design will also fit a standard 3¼in (8cm) diameter coaster, if you omit the tiny corner motifs.

**Colour key**

| | | Anchor | DMC | Madeira | Strands for cross stitch | Strands for backstitch | Amount |
|---|---|---|---|---|---|---|---|
| | Very pale blue | 128 | 3753 | 1001 | 2 | 1 | 0.5m (1½ft) |
| | Pale blue | 131 | 798 | 0911 | 2 | – | 0.5m (1½ft) |
| | Darkish blue | 134 | 820 | 0913 | 2 | 1 | 0.5m (1½ft) |

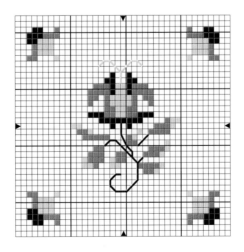

# POT HOLDER

This small design is the prettiest way I can think of to give
a warning that something will be hot, and that care needs to be taken!
I have used wavy lines of backstitch to suggest heat rising
from the freshly baked pie, and more backstitch detail on
the pastry rim to suggest a forked edge.

**Design size**
3 x 2½in (7.5 x 6.3cm) on 14 count
**Stitch count**
41 x 35
**Materials**
Ready-made pot holder, 8in (20cm) square,
with cream, 14 count Aida corner to stitch on
Threads as listed in the colour key
Size 24 tapestry needle

# WORKING THE DESIGN

Start in the centre of the design, which is just at the top of the pastry leaves. Stitch the pastry first, then the pattern on the dish. Work the outline of the pie dish, then 'colour in' the background, using kingfisher blue. When all the cross stitch is complete, work the backstitch on the pie itself, and the steam above it, with the appropriate colour.

# VARIATIONS

I stitched this motif on a square, ready-made pot holder, but it would be equally suitable worked on the backs of a pair of oven gloves, or either end of an oven mitt.

## Colour key

| | | Anchor | DMC | Madeira | Strands for cross stitch | Strands for backstitch | Amount |
|---|---|---|---|---|---|---|---|
| | Green | 215 | 320 | 1311 | 2 | – | 0.5m (1½ft) |
| | Lemon | 292 | 3078 | 0111 | 2 | – | 0.5m (1½ft) |
| | Chocolate brown | 357 | 300 | 2304 | – | 1 | 0.5m (1½ft) |
| | Brown | 365 | 435 | 2010 | 2 | 1 | 0.5m (1½ft) |
| | Light gold | 368 | 436 | 2013 | 2 | – | 1m (1yd) |
| | Kingfisher blue | 940 | 798 | 0905 | 2 | – | 1.5m (1yd 2ft) |

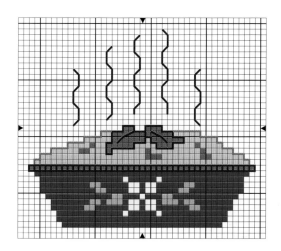

# FOUR

# CRACKER PLACEMAT

Christmas crackers really liven up the festive table with their bright colours and promise of a small gift. However, they seem to become more and more expensive every year, and the contents always seem a disappointment! By stitching a cracker on each placemat, you can have the best of both worlds – a beautiful table decoration, which cannot outshine its contents, as there aren't any!

**Design size**
16 x 10¼in (40.5 x 26cm) on 14 count
**Stitch count**
223 x 143
**Materials**
Christmas green, 14 count Aida,
20 x 15in (50 x 38cm)
Threads as listed in the colour key
Size 24 tapestry needle

## WORKING THE DESIGN

Start by finding the centre of your fabric, then measure 6in (15cm) to the left to find the centre of the cracker motif itself. This is where to start stitching. Work the floral rosette motif first, and then the main body of the cracker. To work the border, count out blank squares from the edge of the cracker motif to the inner line of the border pattern. How many squares you need to count depends on where you choose to start from. The shortest distance between stitched areas is usually the best policy. When all the cross stitch is completed, go back over the design working all the backstitch to give definition. If you do not want to use gold thread on this design, a gold-coloured embroidery silk will do instead.

## FINISHING

Your placemat can be finished either by hemming the edge, or fringing it. For instructions on hemming, see Hemming, page 129, and for fringing see the finishing instructions for the Poppy Placemat on page 42.

## VARIATIONS

A simple variation of this design would be to alter the colour of the fabric, and the main colour of the cracker itself, so that each guest has a unique placemat. Reversing the green fabric/red cracker combination would look good. Navy Aida also looks 'Christmassy', as does black, surprisingly. You could create a matching tablecloth for your placemats quite simply, by working four cracker motifs in a square in the centre of the cloth, and then working a border of crackers around the hem.

| Colour key | | Anchor | DMC | Madeira | Strands for cross stitch | Strands for backstitch | Amount |
|---|---|---|---|---|---|---|---|
| | White | 1 | Blanc | White | 2 | – | 1m (1yd) |
| | Maroon | 22 | 814 | 0514 | 2 | 1 | 1.5m (1yd 2ft) |
| | Bright red | 47 | 321 | 0509 | 2 | – | 5.5m (6yd) |
| | Metallic gold (Balger) | 102 | 102 | 102 | 1 | 1 | 2.5m (2yd 2ft) |
| | Royal blue | 133 | 797 | 0913 | 2 | – | 1m (1yd) |

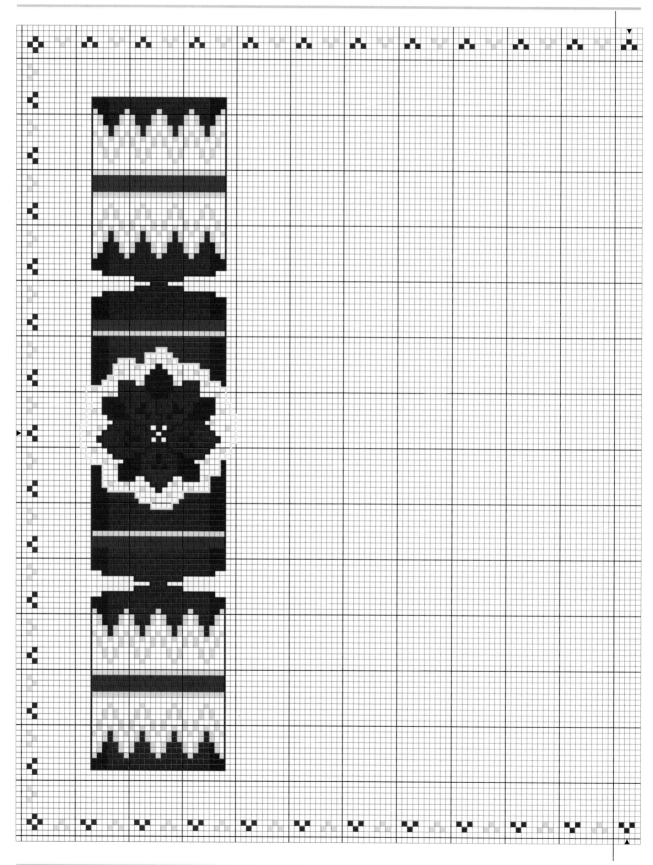

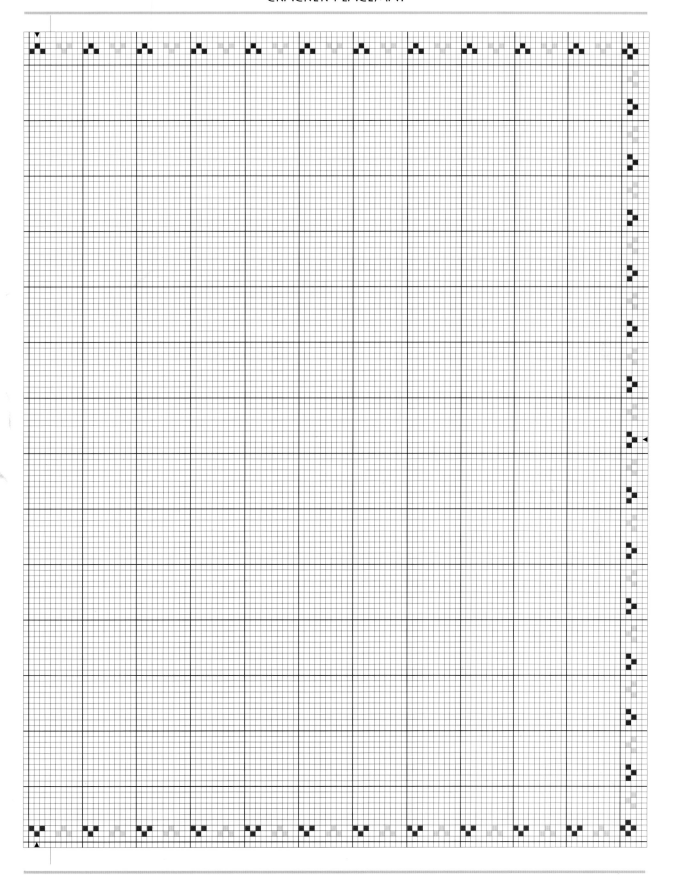

# CRACKER PLACECARDS

These small motifs can quickly be worked, to add a personal touch to your Christmas table. They co-ordinate well with the Cracker Placemat on page 78, but can be used independently equally well. I have mounted these placecards in bookmark mounts and stood them on their long edge, left unglued. Using the mounts I have chosen, along with the alphabet given here, you will have 25 stitches of space for the name, which is enough for about eight letters. For longer names, you could design your own smaller alphabet on graph paper, or move the 'cracker end' motifs out slightly. Plan the lettering before you begin stitching, so you don't end up with a nasty surprise if it doesn't all fit!

⊠

**Design size (each motif)**
3¾ x 1in (9.5 x 2.5cm) on 14 count
**Stitch count**
63 x 14
**Materials (for each placecard)**
Various colours, such as red, green, black, white
and navy, 14 count Aida, 2½ x 6in (6.5 x 15cm)
Bookmark mounts, 7 x 2in (18 x 5cm)
with rectangular apertures of 1¼ x 5¼
(3.2 x 13.5cm) (maximum) in various colours
to contrast with the fabric
Threads as listed in the colour key
Size 24 tapestry needle

## WORKING THE DESIGN

Plan your lettering first, leaving one blank square between each letter. Stitch the name first in backstitch, starting in the centre and working outwards. Then work each half of the cracker in cross stitch, going back over the design to do the backstitch outlining last.

## FINISHING

To make up the placecards, first trim your fabric to a little less than 7 x 2in (18 x 5cm), and iron it on the wrong side, on a padded board. On the reverse of the mount's centre panel, place strips of double-sided tape around the opening, and also around the very edges of the centre panel (see Fig 9). The fabric should be cut carefully to fit within the tape stuck around the edges of the centre panel, so that there is not too much bulk. Check the assembly of the placecard to make sure that the fabric will definitely fit, then remove the backing paper from the tape. With the fabric placed face up on the table, lower the panel onto the stitching, checking that it is centred. Fold the third of the mount which is nearest to you underneath the centre panel, then press gently, but firmly to fix the two layers together, completing your placecard.

**Fig 9. Mounting fabric in 'placecards'
(i.e. bookmark mounts).**

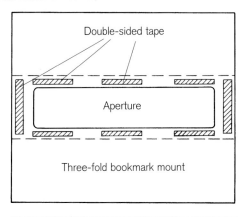

Double-sided tape
Aperture
Three-fold bookmark mount

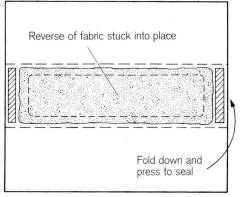

Reverse of fabric stuck into place
Fold down and press to seal

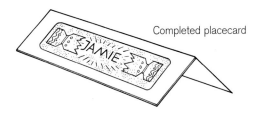

Completed placecard

## VARIATIONS

These placecards can be given to your guests for them to use as personalized bookmarks, by simply sticking down the remaining panel. They can also be converted into name tags for Christmas presents, by punching a hole in one corner of the card mount. Make sure, however, that the fabric has been trimmed far enough in from the edge first, as a hole punch will not cut through fabric. The cracker motif would also look good worked on Aida band, perhaps in a lower count, and slip-stitched onto a child's Christmas sack or stocking – or any Christmas item that can be personalized.

## Colour key

| | | Anchor | DMC | Madeira | Strands for cross stitch | Strands for backstitch | Amount |
|---|---|---|---|---|---|---|---|
| | Maroon | 22 | 814 | 0514 | – | 1 | 0.5m (1½ft) |
| | Bright red | 47 | 321 | 0509 | 2 | 1 | 1m (1yd) |
| | Metallic gold (Balger) | 102 | 102 | 102 | 1 | – | 0.5m (1½ft) |
| | Royal blue | 133 | 797 | 0913 | 2 | – | 1m (1yd) |
| | Bright grass green | 229 | 700 | 1304 | 2 | – | 1m (1yd) |

**NB:** a single strand of any of the above shades, or black, can be used for the lettering.

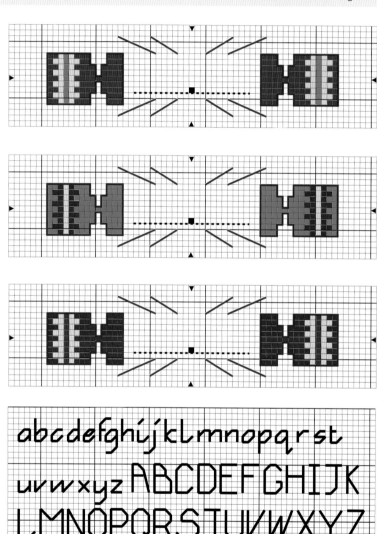

# CHRISTMAS MOUSE COASTER

Black is a surprisingly good colour to use in Christmas designs:
it is so dramatic, and bright red and green stand out well against it.
In this design, I have used it as a backing for a mouse
hanging up her Christmas stocking.

## Design size
2½ x 2½in (6.4 x 6.4cm) on 14 count
## Stitch count
36 x 35
## Materials
Black, 14 count Aida, 6 x 6in (15 x 15cm)
Clear acrylic coaster 3¼in (8cm)
Threads as listed in the colour key
Size 24 tapestry needle

# WORKING THE DESIGN

Starting in the centre of the design, work the mouse's clothes first. You will probably find it easier to work the dots on the dress before stitching the cream background fabric. Once this is done, stitch the grey head, tail and legs, before finally stitching the Christmas stocking. Work the backstitch outlining once all the cross stitch is completed.

# FINISHING

Separate the two halves of the coaster, and place the top disc on the fabric, centring the design. Mark around the edge using a pencil (on fabric this dark you may need to use tailors' chalk so that the line shows up), then cut just inside this line so that the fabric fits the coaster snugly. Place the paper disc that comes with the coaster back into the base of the coaster mount first, to neaten the back of your stitching, then put the fabric into the mount, and finally, fix the clear plastic top disc.

# VARIATIONS

By changing around some of the colours used for the mouse's clothes and stocking, you could make a set of coasters, all slightly different. The design is also small enough to make a good Christmas card, or even a Christmas present tag for a special friend or relative.

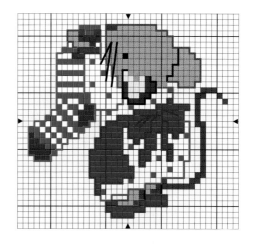

| Colour key | | Anchor | DMC | Madeira | Strands for cross stitch | Strands for backstitch | Amount |
|---|---|---|---|---|---|---|---|
| | White | 1 | Blanc | White | 2 | – | 0.5m (1½ft) |
| | Strawberry red | 46 | 666 | 0210 | 2 | – | 1m (1yd) |
| | Pale rose | 48 | 3713 | 0607 | 2 | – | 0.5m (1½ft) |
| | Bottle green | 211 | 561 | 1313 | 2 | 1 | 0.5m (1½ft) |
| | Cream | 386 | 3823 | 0101 | 2 | – | 1m (1yd) |
| | Light grey | 398 | 415 | 1802 | 2 | – | 1m (1yd) |
| | Dark grey | 400 | 317 | 1714 | 2 | 1 | 0.5m (1½ft) |
| | Black | 403 | 310 | Black | 2 | 1 | 0.5m (1½ft) |
| | Brick red | 897 | 902 | 0601 | 2 | 1 | 0.5m (1½ft) |

# CHRISTMAS CAKEBAND

These simple Christmas motifs are livened up with metallic thread and beads. The thread – lamé embroidery thread – is made up from 12 thin strands, which can be combined to make various thicknesses, just like ordinary stranded cotton. It helps to use multiples of two threads in your needle, as then you can use the 'knotless method' for starting each length of thread (see Starting and Finishing Threads, page 9). When using a single strand, you can knot the thread to the eye of the needle. The knot will be so tiny that it shouldn't interfere with the needle's passing through the fabric.

**Design size**
2 x 30in (5 x 76cm), to fit a 9in (23cm) cake
**Stitch count**
28 high x length as necessary
**Materials**
Christmas red, 14 count Aida band,
2in (5cm)
Fine sewing needle for attaching beads
Dressmakers' pins for attaching band to cake
(remember to remove all pins before
cutting the cake!)
Invisible nylon sewing thread
Threads as listed in the colour key
Size 24 tapestry needle

# WORKING THE DESIGN

Usually, a design is begun in the centre of the fabric, but in this case it is more sensible to start at one end of the band and work along it systematically. Work the cross stitches for each motif first, as usual, then the beads, applying them with invisible nylon sewing thread (available from haberdashery departments).

When using beads, always use a fine sewing needle (called a 'sharp'), rather than a tapestry needle, as the beads have a very small hole. Make sure that the thread is securely fixed at the back of your work, then pick up a bead and attach it using a half cross stitch, worked in the same direction as the top diagonal of your whole cross stitches. This will give a neat and consistent appearance to your work. Finish off each length and start again rather than jumping across any gaps larger than about ½in (1cm), as the thread may become slack, causing the beads to appear to be falling off your fabric! If you prefer, you could leave out the beads and use shades of thread (either metallic or stranded cotton) to replace them. If practical, keep trying the cakeband on the cake to ensure that you don't work more motifs than necessary.

# FINISHING

Turn each short end under ¼in (0.75cm), and neaten with slip stitch. Position on the cake and hold in place using the dressmakers' pins.

## Colour key

| | | Anchor | DMC | Madeira | Strands for cross stitch | Strands for backstitch | Amount |
|---|---|---|---|---|---|---|---|
| | White | 1 | Blanc | White | 2 | – | 4.5m (4yd 3ft) |
| | Sand | 288 | 445 | 0103 | 2 | – | 2m (2yd 6in) |
| | Bright yellow | 291 | 444 | 0105 | 2 | 1 | 1m (1yd) |
| | Orange | 316 | 971 | 0202 | 2 | – | 0.5m (1½ft) |
| | Royal blue lamé | 320 | 826 | 1102 | 2 | 1 | 2m (2yd 6in) |
| | Christmas green lamé | 322 | 702 | 1403 | 2 | – | 4.5m (4yd 3ft) |
| | Coffee bean brown | 381 | 938 | 2006 | 2 | – | 0.5m (1½ft) |
| | Black | 403 | 310 | Black | 2 | 1 | 1.5m (1yd 2ft) |
| | Mill Hill seed beads (Victoria Gold 00557) | | | | | | 90 beads |

Beginning of pattern repeat →

## VARIATIONS

To continue the theme of the small Christmas motifs, you could make placecards using scraps of Aida band with one motif worked on the left-hand side, and the person's name stitched (using backstitch) on the right.

Neaten the fabric and attach to a piece of folded card with double-sided tape. Matching napkin rings could also be made, using more Aida band scraps: simply work the motif and then, with right sides in, sew the two short sides together to make a ring.

# FIVE

TOPIARY CURTAIN
TIE-BACKS
FESTIVE WREATH
TABLECLOTH
JAM POT COVERS
BABY'S BIB
WITH CLOWN MOTIF
KEY RACK

# TOPIARY CURTAIN TIE-BACKS

Topiary is the art of clipping plants into artificial, but aesthetic, shapes. They can be formal or humorous, and always add a sculptural quality to a garden. As curtains frame a view of the outside world, I felt that a garden theme would be appropriate for this pair of tie-backs.

⊠ ⊠
**Design size (each)**
21 x 5¼in (58 x 13.5cm) on 14 count
**Stitch count (each)**
293 x 71
**Materials (for one pair of tie-backs)**
Cream, 14 count Aida, 16 x 27in (40 x 70cm)
Iron-on interlining, 16 x 27in (40 x 70cm)
Cream cotton backing fabric, 16 x 27in (40 x 70cm)
Brass or strong plastic curtain rings x 4,
1in (2.5cm) diameter
Threads as listed in the colour key
Size 24 tapestry needle

## WORKING THE DESIGN

Using the black outline on page 130 as a guide, make a paper pattern for your tie-backs and try this against your curtains. (The template is full size, but shows half the pattern only.) If necessary, adjust the length by taking off or adding paper at the centre of the pattern. If you do adjust the length, you will need to decide whether to add or subtract one or two topiary trees. Plan this before you start stitching! Beware of making the tie-backs too short, or your curtains will become creased. Once you have determined the correct size, pin the paper pattern onto one half of your Aida, and mark around the edge with tailors' chalk. Move the pattern onto the remaining half – leaving a gap of at least 2in (5cm) – and mark around the outline again. Then, working from the centre of each tie-back outwards, begin the cross stitch topiary. It will look

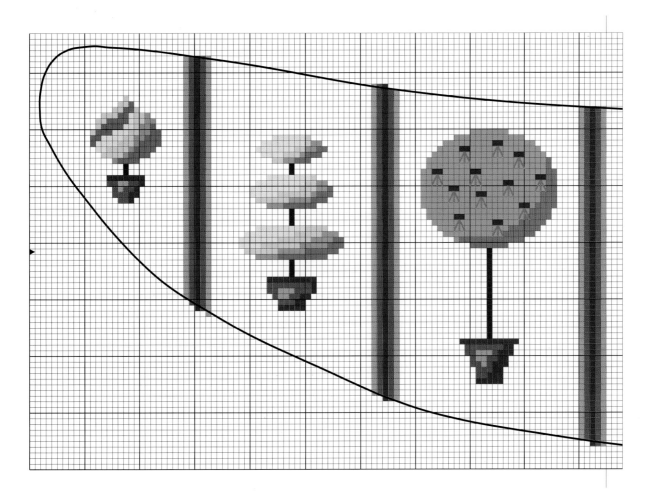

neater when made up if you extend the terracotta stripes a little way past your drawn outline. This way, when your tie-back is hemmed and turned, the stripes will definitely reach the edges. For each plant, count out where the pot should be and work this first, then stitch the trunk, and finally the topiary itself. When all the cross stitching is complete, work the stamens of the fuchsia flowers on the 'lollipop tree' in cherry pink.

## Colour key

| | | Anchor | DMC | Madeira | Strands for cross stitch | Strands for backstitch | Amount |
|---|---|---|---|---|---|---|---|
| | Cherry pink | 54 | 956 | 0413 | – | 1 | 0.5m (1½ft) |
| | Cranberry | 59 | 326 | 0603 | 2 | – | 0.5m (1½ft) |
| | Light moss green | 254 | 3348 | 1409 | 2 | – | 3m (3yd 1ft) |
| | Moss green | 256 | 906 | 1411 | 2 | – | 5m (5yd 1½ft) |
| | Dark moss green | 258 | 904 | 1413 | 2 | – | 3.5m (3yd 2½ft) |
| | Pastel green | 259 | 772 | 1604 | 2 | – | 2.5m (2yd 2ft) |
| | Pale orange | 336 | 758 | 2313 | 2 | – | 4.5m (4yd 3ft) |
| | Terracotta | 338 | 356 | 0402 | 2 | – | 4.5m (4yd 3ft) |
| | Dark terracotta | 341 | 3777 | 0401 | 2 | – | 3m (3yd 1ft) |
| | Henna brown | 380 | 938 | 2005 | 2 | – | 1.5m (1yd 2ft) |

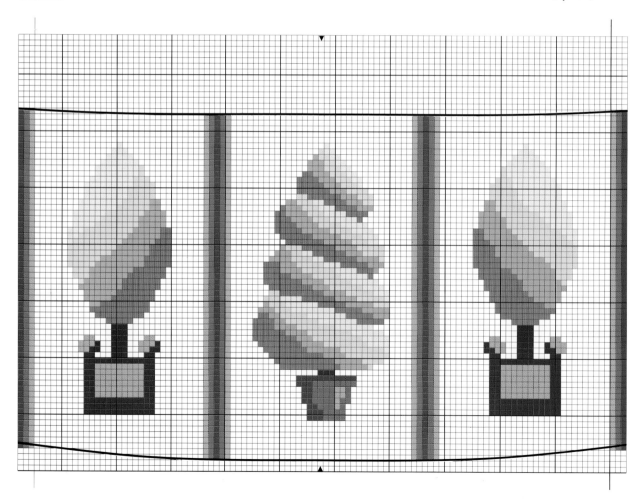

96

## FINISHING

Trim each tie-back to within ½in (1cm) of the outline (as printed on the chart). Cut a piece of interlining, and a piece of backing fabric to the same size. Iron the interlining to the reverse of the stitched fabric. Place the stitched fabric and backing fabric right sides together, and sew around the edge of the tie-back, leaving a gap of 3in (7cm) to allow for turning through (see Fig 10).

**Fig 10. Completing the tie-back.**

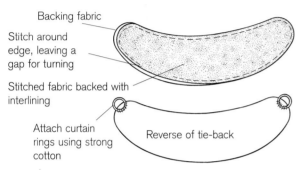

Backing fabric

Stitch around edge, leaving a gap for turning

Stitched fabric backed with interlining

Attach curtain rings using strong cotton

Reverse of tie-back

Clip along the curves every ½in (1cm) or so up to the sewn line, then turn through so that the right sides are facing out, and press. Clipping the curves reduces bulk when the tie-back is turned right side out, and so gives a smoother finished line. Finally, slip stitch the opening shut, and attach a curtain ring at either end of the tie-back, using strong sewing cotton (see Fig 10).

## VARIATIONS

For a really co-ordinated look, work a 4in (10cm) Aida band with the topiary trees, and slip stitch it to a piece of fabric to make a pelmet. The same width Aida band attached to the bottom of a roller blind would also look very smart. You will need to adjust the positions of the topiary trees slightly so that the base of all the plant pots are level. To ensure that the light shining through your work from the back doesn't show up the reverse of your stitching, keep all loose threads trimmed close, and do not jump across areas – fasten off and start again!

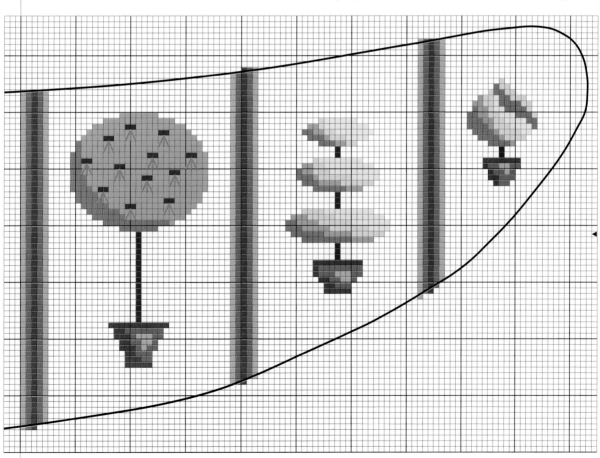

# FESTIVE WREATH TABLECLOTH

A festive table should always impress, and this design certainly does that. The wreath motif is worked four times around the centre point of the cloth, leaving a blank area, so that you can place a decoration or candle in the middle without covering up any stitching. The small motifs between the wreaths will help you count across from one wreath to the next. Remember, if you turn your cloth through 90° to work each wreath the 'right way up', the top stitch of each cross stitch must slope in the same direction across the whole design.

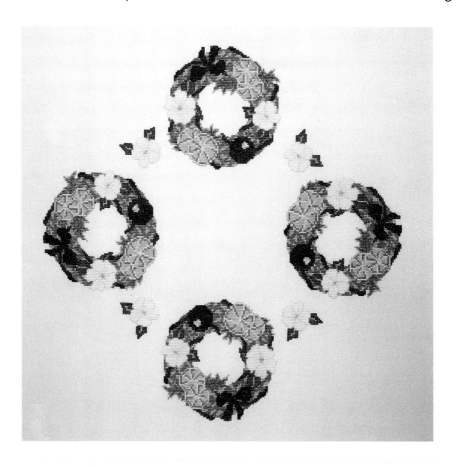

⊠ ⊠ ⊠

### Design size
Total 17 x 17in (43 x 43cm)
One wreath motif only 5½ x 5½in (14 x 14cm)
### Stitch count
Total 238 x 238
One wreath motif only 78 x 78
### Materials
Cream, 28 count Linda evenweave fabric,
52 x 52in (132 x 132cm)
Threads as listed in the colour key
Size 24 tapestry needle

## WORKING THE DESIGN

Fold the fabric in half and in half again to find the centre, and mark this spot with a pin. Measure out 2¾in (7cm) from this point along one thread of the cloth to find the centre top of the first wreath motif and start stitching from here. Work the main elements of the wreath first – the orange slices, the Christmas roses, bow and bauble – then work the narrow red ribbon. The foliage 'body' of the wreath is then much easier to stitch. Once all the cross stitching is complete, work the backstitch outlining and detail in the appropriate colour. You may prefer to completely finish each wreath before going on to the next. Stitch the individual Christmas roses and leaves in the spaces between the wreaths in the same way – cross stitch first, then backstitch details.

## FINISHING

For details of how to hem your tablecloth, see Hemming, page 129.

## VARIATIONS

The single Christmas rose motifs would look lovely stitched on the corners of matching napkins, or repeated around a cakeband. Or you could try stitching the whole of one wreath motif singly, and mounting it as a cushion, framed in a deep border of red velvet.

## Colour key

| | | Anchor | DMC | Madeira | Strands for cross stitch | Strands for backstitch | Amount |
|---|---|---|---|---|---|---|---|
| | Dark Christmas red | 44 | 814 | 0514 | 2 | – | 8.5m (9yd 1ft) |
| | Bright red | 47 | 321 | 0509 | 2 | – | 4m (4yd 1ft) |
| | Pale rose | 48 | 3713 | 0607 | 2 | – | 1.5m (1yd 2ft) |
| | Pink | 74 | 3689 | 0606 | 2 | 1 | 1.5m (1yd 2ft) |
| | Very dark green | 218 | 319 | 1405 | – | 1 | 1m (1yd) |
| | Olive green | 265 | 3348 | 1603 | 2 | – | 2m (2yd 6in) |
| | Light green | 267 | 469 | 1503 | 2 | – | 9m (9yd 2ft 6in) |
| | Light yellow | 300 | 745 | 0111 | 2 | – | 12.5m (13yd 2ft) |
| | Pale yellow | 301 | 744 | 0112 | 2 | – | 5.5m (6yd) |
| | Pale orange | 336 | 758 | 2313 | 2 | – | 6.5m (7yd 6in) |
| | Terracotta | 338 | 356 | 0402 | 2 | 1 | 4.5m (4yd 3ft) |
| | Golden yellow | 362 | 437 | 2012 | 2 | – | 0.5m (1½ ft) |
| | Palest green | 858 | 524 | 1511 | 2 | – | 6.5m (7yd 6in) |
| | Pale forest green | 860 | 3363 | 1513 | 2 | – | 6.5m (7yd 6in) |
| | Leaf green | 878 | 501 | 1313 | 2 | – | 4.5m (4yd 3ft) |
| | Brick red | 897 | 902 | 0601 | 2 | 1 | 2m (2yd 6in) |

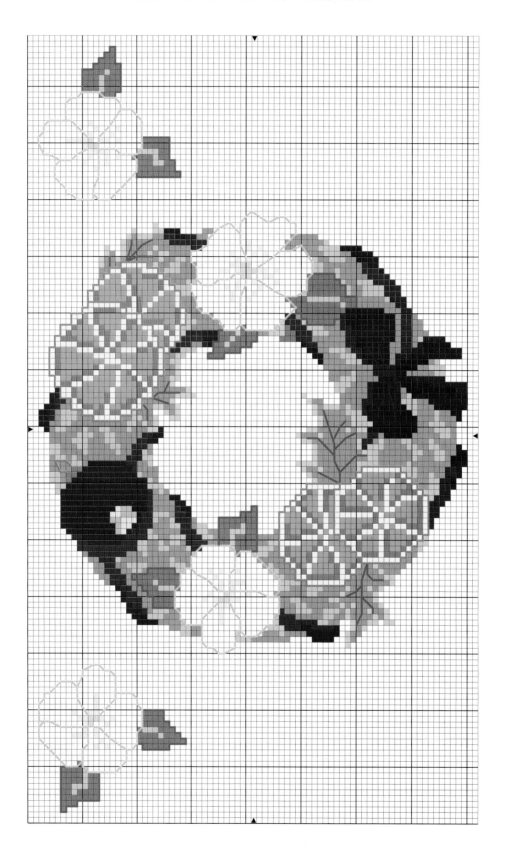

# JAM POT COVERS

Jam making is a skill that is becoming rarer these days. However, it is still worth the effort of making some special recipe for a friend, and finishing off the present with a hand-stitched cover. If you don't go in for jam making, you could always cheat – buy a jar or two in your local supermarket and soak off the label to make it look more 'home-made'! These three covers have been designed using colours which give a clue as to their contents. The red/pink one is for strawberry jam, the green/purple one for apple and blackberry jam, and the orange one for marmalade.

⊠

**Design size (each)**
2 x 2in (5 x 5cm) on 18 count
**Stitch count**
35 x 35
**Materials**
'Jar lacies', 7in (18cm), with cream,
18 count Aida centre panels of 3in (7.5cm) x 3
Narrow ribbon pieces in suitable colours,
to tie around jars, 1m (1yd)
Threads as listed in colour keys
Size 26 needle

# WORKING THE DESIGNS

Carefully measure to the centre of each Aida panel, and begin stitching from there. Work the more solid blocks of colour for each design first, then the contrasting 'dots' of colour. Finally, work any backstitch in the appropriate shade.

# FINISHING

Thread the narrow ribbon through the holes in the lace. Put the lacy over the jar and gather the ribbon up, making a bow to hold it in place.

# VARIATIONS

If the jar of jam is for a present, you could work the design again, this time on a plain piece of Aida, and make it into a gift tag.

### Colour key for strawberry jam pot cover

| | | Anchor | DMC | Madeira | Strands for cross stitch | Strands for backstitch | Amount |
|---|---|---|---|---|---|---|---|
| ■ | Red | 19 | 304 | 0510 | 2 | 1 | 0.5m (1½ft) |
| ▨ | Medium pink | 24 | 776 | 0503 | 2 | – | 1m (1yd) |
| ☐ | Cream | 386 | 3823 | 0101 | 2 | – | 0.5m (1½ft) |

### Colour key for apple and blackberry jam pot cover

| | | Anchor | DMC | Madeira | Strands for cross stitch | Strands for backstitch | Amount |
|---|---|---|---|---|---|---|---|
| ▨ | Sugar pink | 49 | 963 | 0607 | 2 | – | 0.5m (1½ft) |
| ■ | Dark purple | 102 | 550 | 0714 | 2 | – | 1m (1yd) |
| ■ | Foliage green | 263 | 3362 | 1507 | 2 | – | 0.5m (1½ft) |
| ▨ | Yellow green | 264 | 3348 | 1604 | 2 | – | 0.5m (1½ft) |

### Colour key for marmalade pot cover

| | | Anchor | DMC | Madeira | Strands for cross stitch | Strands for backstitch | Amount |
|---|---|---|---|---|---|---|---|
| ☐ | Lemon | 292 | 3078 | 0111 | 2 | – | 0.5m (1½ft) |
| ▨ | Pale terracotta | 313 | 3825 | 0114 | 2 | – | 0.5m (1½ft) |
| ■ | Orange | 316 | 971 | 0202 | 2 | – | 0.5m (1½ft) |
| ■ | Dark orange | 333 | 606 | 0209 | 2 | 1 | 0.5m (1½ft) |

**Strawberry jam pot cover.**

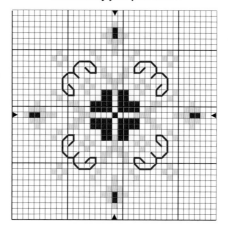

**Blackberry jam pot cover.**

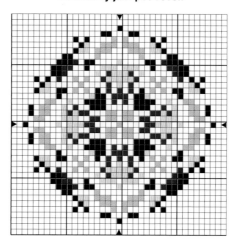

**Marmalade pot cover.**

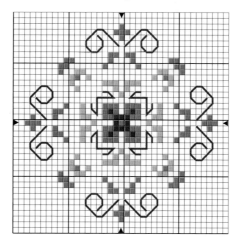

# BABY'S BIB WITH CLOWN MOTIF

This bright and jolly clown must be announcing that dinner is ready!
A lively and colourful picture such as this will appeal to babies, and,
perhaps, the doting aunts and grannies who might have more time
to stitch it than the baby's mum!

**Design size**
2 x 3¾in (5 x 9.5cm) on 14 count
**Stitch count**
28 x 53
**Materials**
Ready-made bib in white, 14 count Aida, with
anglais trim, 7in (18cm) diameter (maximum)
Threads as listed in the colour key
Size 24 needle

## WORKING THE DESIGN

Carefully measure to the centre of the bib, and start
stitching from here. Work the clown's body first, then
the drum and finally the head. When all the cross
stitch is complete, work the tiny bits of backstitch for
the clown's fingers and the folds on the ruff.

## VARIATIONS

This is one of those designs where it is simple to
substitute colours if you don't happen to have the
ones that I suggest: there is no 'correct' colour for a
clown, anything bright will do! There is also space
around the design for you to add the child's name if
you wish. Plan it on graph paper first, then add the
lettering around the edge of the bib.

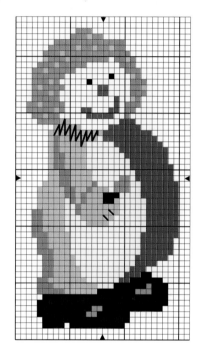

**Colour key**

| | | Anchor | DMC | Madeira | Strands for cross stitch | Strands for backstitch | Amount |
|---|---|---|---|---|---|---|---|
| | Strawberry red | 46 | 666 | 0210 | 2 | – | 0.5m (1½ft) |
| | Pale blue | 131 | 798 | 0911 | 2 | – | 0.5m (1½ft) |
| | Canvas green | 246 | 895 | 1404 | 2 | – | 1m (1yd) |
| | Moss green | 256 | 906 | 1411 | 2 | – | 0.5m (1½ft) |
| | Yellow | 289 | 307 | 0103 | 2 | – | 1m (1yd) |
| | Pale terracotta | 313 | 3825 | 0114 | 2 | – | 0.5m (1½ft) |
| | Mandarin | 324 | 721 | 0309 | 2 | – | 1m (1yd) |
| | Light grey | 398 | 415 | 1802 | 2 | – | 0.5m (1½ft) |
| | Dark grey | 400 | 317 | 1714 | 2 | 1 | 1m (1yd) |
| | Black | 403 | 310 | Black | 2 | – | 0.5m (1½ft) |
| | Purple blue | 977 | 334 | 1711 | 2 | – | 1m (1yd) |

# KEY RACK

'A place for everything and everything in its place' is a good saying, but not one that is easy to put into practice. Keys have a habit of being dumped on the first surface that is reached after entering the house – they then become covered up by newspapers, letters, or whatever. Why not stitch this key rack, so that all your keys are safe and easy to find?

## Design size
6½ x 3¼in (16.5 x 8cm) on 14 count
## Stitch count
93 x 43
## Materials
White, 14 count Aida, 6 x 11in (15 x 28cm)
Wooden picture frame, 6 x 8in (15 x 20cm),
with five brass cup hooks fixed evenly along
the bottom edge
Brass key 'charms'
Threads as listed in the colour key
Size 24 tapestry needle

# WORKING THE DESIGN
Starting in the centre of the design, work the gold
scroll pattern for the barrel of the key. It will be easier
to stitch with the gold filament if you knot it to the
needle, as it is so fine a thread. Fill in around the gold

with black, using two strands, and then work the
lettering, the oval shape and the filigree pattern at the
end of the key. Finally, outline the lettering and the
filigree design with a single strand of gold.

Attach the key charms randomly around the key
motif, using strong sewing thread. You may need to
'seal' the surface of the charms first, using acrylic
lacquer, to prevent them discolouring.

# FINISHING
Frame the design as you would a picture, referring to
Mounting and Framing, page 129.

# VARIATIONS
One variation you could try is to allocate each brass
hook to a particular set of keys, by adding the owner's
name above their hook. Use the Cracker Placecard
alphabet on page 84, or the Strawberry Jam Sampler
letters on page 114. Alternatively, you could stitch
small pictures to represent the relevant item that the
key locks – for instance, a car, or a garden shed.

## Colour key

| | | Anchor | DMC | Madeira | Strands for cross stitch | Strands for backstitch | Amount |
|---|---|---|---|---|---|---|---|
| | Metallic gold | 192 | 102 | 102 | 1 | 1 | 2m (2yd 6in) |
| | Black | 310 | 403 | Black | 2 | 1 | 4m (4yd 1ft) |

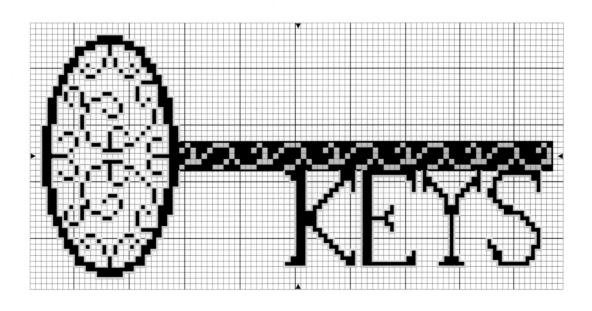

RECIPE FOR
STRAWBERRY JAM

Ingredients
2½ lb strawberries
3lb 2oz preserving sugar
3 tablespoonsful fresh lemon juice

Method
Put the strawberries and sugar
together in a preserving pan, over a
low heat, stirring until they are
well mixed. Continue cooking until
the fruit is soft and the sugar
dissolved; then raise the heat. Add
the lemon juice and boil fast for
10 to 15 minutes, on until it sets
when tested. Bottle in clean, hot
jars, cover with parchment, and
label. (Makes approx. 4 lb.)

# SIX

# STRAWBERRY JAM RECIPE SAMPLER

The inspiration for this design came from my own strawberry plants.
They were given to me as rooted cuttings – now they are threatening to take
over the whole bed, they are so prolific! It is always a joy to lift a leaf and find
a cluster of ripening strawberries nestling underneath. Once they are ripe,
there are suddenly too many to know what to do with – making jam is one
solution. Having stitched this design, you could go on to make the jam,
and even use the Jam Pot Covers on page 101 to decorate your jars.

**Design size**
9¾ x 14½ (25 x 37cm) on 14 count
**Stitch count**
137 x 203
**Materials**
Mint green, 14 count Aida, 14 x 20in (35.5 x 50cm)
Wooden frame, 12 x 16in (30 x 41cm) (minimum);
larger if you also use a card mount
Threads as listed in the colour key
Size 24 tapestry needle

## WORKING THE DESIGN

Starting in the centre of the design, work all the lettering, using one strand of very dark brown. Underline the headings with a single row of cross stitch. Stitch the strawberry border next, starting with the top leaf motif and working out and down the design. Take care over the placing of the strawberries up the sides. Work the bottom centre motif last. Once all the cross stitch is complete, work the backstitch, outlining the leaves and strawberries, and adding veins to the leaves where indicated.

## FINISHING

For information on how to frame pictures, see Mounting and Framing, page 129.

## VARIATIONS

A row of the individual strawberries can be stitched onto almost any small kitchen item. Stitched on a shelf edging they would look eye-catching, or how about a tea towel? If you have a narrow scrap of fabric left over, a vertical row of strawberries would make a good bookmark for a recipe book. For an alternative project, you could leave out the lettering, but work the border as given. When mounting it, fix a piece of corkboard in the centre to make a memo board.

| Colour key | | Anchor | DMC | Madeira | Strands for cross stitch | Strands for backstitch | Amount |
|---|---|---|---|---|---|---|---|
| | Deep red | 20 | 815 | 0512 | 2 | – | 4m (4yd 1ft) |
| | Strawberry red | 46 | 666 | 0210 | 2 | – | 6m (6yd 1½ft) |
| | Light green | 267 | 469 | 1503 | 2 | – | 6.5m (7yd 6in) |
| | Dark green | 269 | 936 | 1507 | 2 | 1 | 2.5m (2yd 2ft) |
| | Chocolate brown | 357 | 300 | 2304 | 2 | 1 | 2m (2yd 6in) |
| | Very dark brown | 382 | 3371 | 2004 | 2 | 1 | 4m (4yd 1ft) |

RECIPE FOR
STRAWBERRY JAM

Ingredients
2½ lb strawberries
3 lb 2 oz preserving sugar
3 tablespoonsful fresh lemon juice

Method
Put the strawberries and sugar
together in a preserving pan, over a

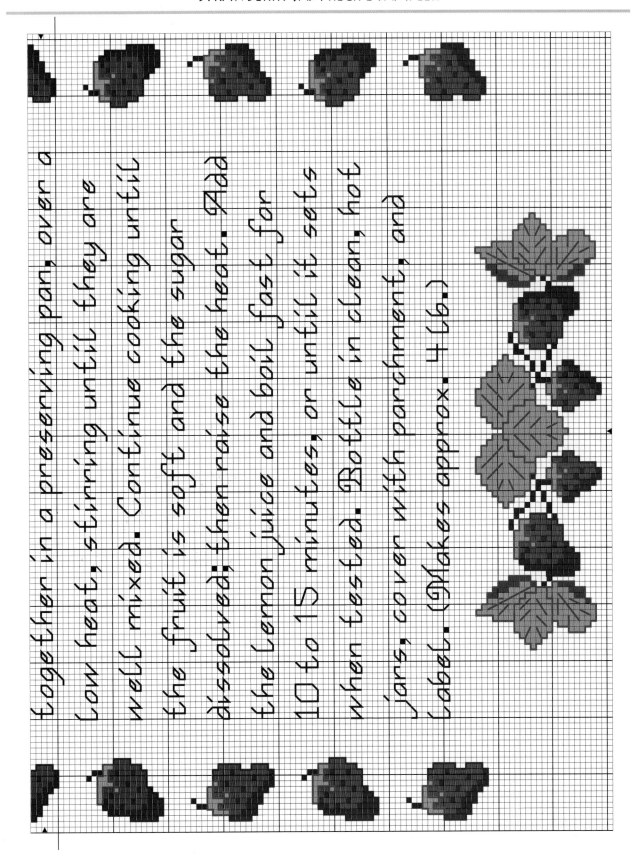

together in a preserving pan, over a

low heat, stirring until they are

well mixed. Continue cooking until

the fruit is soft and the sugar

dissolved; then raise the heat. Add

the lemon juice and boil fast for

10 to 15 minutes, or until it sets

when tested. Bottle in clean, hot

jars, cover with parchment, and

label. (Makes approx. 4 (6.))

# ART DECO
# TEAPOT STAND

This Art Deco pattern is an interpretation in stitches of one of the most popular designs by Clarice Cliff. The design, 'Orange Roof Cottage', was originally created for tableware, for which Clarice Cliff became internationally famous. Her bright, distinctive and unconventional landscapes (as well as her more abstract geometric designs) have become very collectable in recent years – so perhaps the only way to possess something in her style is to stitch your own version! This design is suitable for beginners, and should only take a few evenings to complete.

**Design size**
4¾in (12cm) diameter on 14 count
**Stitch count**
67 x 67
**Materials**
Cream, 14 count Aida, 8 x 8in (20 x 20cm)
Wooden hexagonal teapot stand with heat-resistant
glass and aperture of 4½in (114mm) diameter
Threads as listed in the colour key
Size 24 needle

# WORKING THE DESIGN

Start in the centre by stitching the house and tree, then work outwards and downwards, stitching the areas of 'landscaping'. Work the rings of colour to frame the landscape design. When all the cross stitch is completed, place the teapot stand over the embroidery to make sure that no bare fabric shows around the edges of the design. If it does show slightly, work one more ring of black cross stitches. Finally, work all the backstitch.

# FINISHING

Wash and press your stitching if necessary (see Finishing, page 128). To mount the stitching in the teapot stand, take the circular card template included with the stand and place it over the stitching, making sure that it is centred over the design area. Mark carefully around the template with a pencil or tailors' chalk, then cut out the design using sharp scissors. As the design, once in the mount, will not suffer from any wear, and will be held securely, it is safe to cut very close to the stitched area. Place the fabric in the mount, then use card packing pieces to completely fill the rebated area of the mount – the fabric needs to be pressed close to the heat-resistant glass in order to keep the design looking sharp. Finally, fix the self-adhesive, non-slip base material in place, and your teapot stand is ready for years of use.

# VARIATIONS

This design would look good worked on a higher count fabric to make a smaller finished design suitable for a set of coasters. If you already collect Clarice Cliff tableware, or Art Deco ceramics generally, a set of coasters in this style would really set it off. Alternatively, you could work the design in a circular flexi-hoop and display it on a wall, perhaps mixed with a collection of Art Deco plates?

| Colour key | | Anchor | DMC | Madeira | Strands for cross stitch | Strands for backstitch | Amount |
|---|---|---|---|---|---|---|---|
| | Dusty pink | 95 | 211 | 0801 | 2 | – | 0.5m (1½ft) |
| | Grass green | 209 | 913 | 1212 | 2 | – | 1m (1yd) |
| | Dark yellow | 305 | 743 | 0113 | 2 | – | 3.5m (3yd 2½ft) |
| | Tan | 307 | 783 | 2211 | 2 | – | 1m (1yd) |
| | Orange | 316 | 971 | 0202 | 2 | – | 2.5m (2yd 2ft) |
| | Black | 403 | 310 | Black | 2 | 1 | 4m (4yd 1ft) |
| | Violet | 939 | 793 | 0906 | 2 | – | 1m (1yd) |

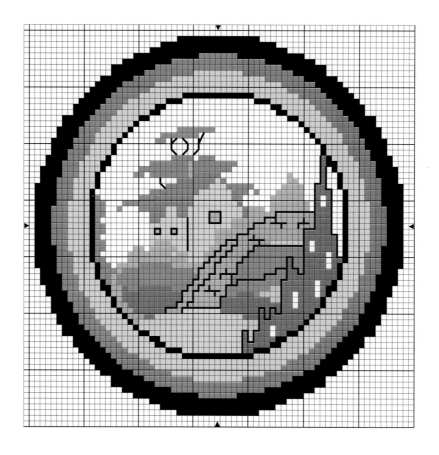

# TEDDY BEAR FRIDGE MAGNETS

This cute 'bear train' will certainly brighten up the fridge door
with its carriage, engine and guard's van, all worked in lively colours.
The friendly bears on the train all wave to the passers-by
– all except the little bear, that is, who is too shy.

**Design size (each)**
2¼ x 1½in (5.5 x 4cm) on 18 count
**Stitch count (largest magnet)**
Stitch count 40 x 29
**Materials (for all three magnets)**
Cream, 18 count Aida, 11 x 5in (28 x 13cm)
Clear plastic fridge magnets,
2 x 3in (5 x 7.5cm)
Iron-on interlining, 11 x 5in (28 x 13cm)
Threads as listed in the colour key
Size 26 needle

## WORKING THE DESIGNS

For each magnet motif, start near the centre, working the train first, with its stripes, then the wheels. After this, work the bears, adding the backstitch lines for the mouth last, in deep brown.

## FINISHING

Wash and press your fabric if necessary (see Finishing, page 128), then iron the interlining to the back of your fabric to help prevent fraying. Place the plastic mount on the fabric and draw a pencil line around it. Make sure that all three motifs are positioned the same distance up from the base of the magnet mount, or it might appear as if part of your train is floating above the rails! Trim the fabric just inside this pencil line, and then slide into place in the mount.

## VARIATIONS

It is easy to make extra carriages for your train, so that the train becomes longer and longer! For other fridge magnets, you could also add a railway platform, with bear passengers waiting for their train. The train motifs themselves could be stitched on a door fingerplate, with a child's name added beneath it, and then fixed horizontally as a name plaque on a bedroom door.

### Colour key for all three magnets

| | | Anchor | DMC | Madeira | Strands for cross stitch | Strands for backstitch | Amount |
|---|---|---|---|---|---|---|---|
| | Strawberry red | 46 | 666 | 0210 | 2 | – | 2m (2yd 6in) |
| | Dusty blue | 132 | 797 | 0912 | 2 | – | 2m (2yd 6in) |
| | Mid-green | 257 | 3346 | 1504 | 2 | – | 2m (2yd 6in) |
| | Autumn gold | 297 | 726 | 0109 | 2 | – | 0.5m (1½ft) |
| | Straw gold | 308 | 782 | 2211 | 2 | – | 2m (2yd 6in) |
| | Deep brown | 310 | 975 | 2214 | 2 | 1 | 0.5m (1½ft) |
| | Black | 403 | 310 | Black | 2 | 1 | 1.5m (1yd 2ft) |
| | Gold | 891 | 676 | 2208 | 2 | – | 1m (1yd) |

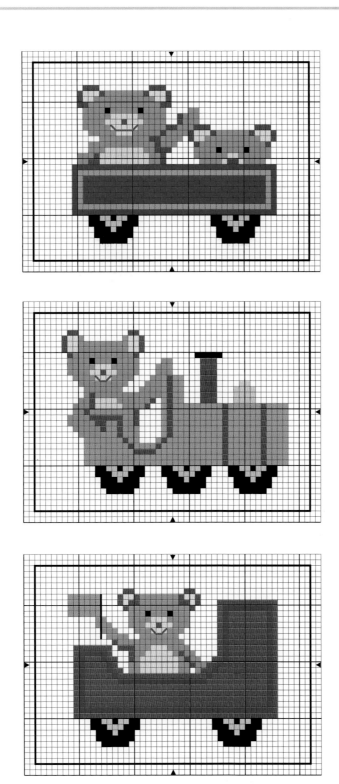

# LETTER RACK

I love getting letters. I feel really put out if the postwoman goes
straight past our house! Surely there must be something for us?
Postboxes often appear on Christmas cards, mainly because of
the idea of contacting loved ones, but also because of the festive
red of postboxes. I have used a speciality Aida cloth for this
project to suggest a cold, snowy landscape. The Aida has a silver
lurex thread running through it, which is perfect for this country
wall postbox, surrounded by frost-covered greenery.

**Design size**
5 x 3in (13 x 7.5cm)
**Stitch count**
71 x 39
**Materials**
Starlite silver, 14 count Aida, 7 x 10in (18 x 25cm)
Wood for letter rack:
Base, 7½ x 3½ x ½in (19 x 9 x 1cm)
Back, 7½ x 7½ x ½in (19 x 19 x 1cm)
Wooden picture frame, 4 x 6in (10 x 15cm)
2oz wadding, 4 x 6in (10 x 15cm)
Threads as listed in the colour key
Size 24 needle

## WORKING THE DESIGN

Start near the centre of the design and work the postbox itself in three shades of red and the 'information plate' in shades of gold and fawn. Next, stitch the greenery tumbling over the wall, and the snow highlights. To give definition to the postbox, add backstitch outlining where indicated, using one strand. Also use one strand of cranberry for the word 'Letters'. Work the rest of the backstitch details – the mortar between the bricks, and the plant stems poking up through the snow – using two strands.

## FINISHING

Using the wooden picture frame, mount the stitching as you would a picture, using wadding under the fabric if you wish (see Mounting and Framing, page 129). Then, take a piece of board, 7½ x 3½ x ½in (19 x 9 x 1cm) for the base, and stand the picture frame on its long edge on the board, ¼in (6mm) back from the front edge, and centred between the two sides. Either glue in place using wood glue, or drill and screw it on. For the back board, take a piece 7½ x 7½ x ½in (19 x 19 x 1cm) and screw or glue it onto the back edge of the baseboard (see Fig 11). Before putting your mounted stitching in the frame, you can either stain the letter rack, or paint it to match your decor.

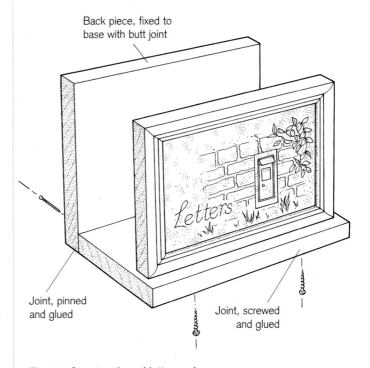

**Fig 11. Construction of letter rack.**

## VARIATIONS

By leaving out the lettering, this design would be very suitable stitched as a Christmas card, especially for someone who lives far away. You could also stitch the design, perhaps on a higher count fabric, such as 22, and mount it in a small box lid, for a special place in which to keep your stamps.

**Colour key**

| | | Anchor | DMC | Madeira | Strands for cross stitch | Strands for backstitch | Amount |
|---|---|---|---|---|---|---|---|
| | Maroon | 22 | 814 | 0514 | 2 | 1 | 0.5m (1½ft) |
| | Strawberry red | 46 | 666 | 0210 | 2 | – | 1m (1yd) |
| | Cranberry | 59 | 326 | 0603 | 2 | 1 | 0.5m (1½ft) |
| | Christmas green | 227 | 701 | 1305 | 2 | – | 0.5m (1½ft) |
| | Canvas green | 246 | 895 | 1404 | 2 | – | 0.5m (1½ft) |
| | Yellow green | 264 | 3348 | 1604 | 2 | – | 0.5m (1½ft) |
| | Hazel | 309 | 780 | 2213 | – | 2 | 0.5m (1½ft) |
| | Oatcake | 388 | 842 | 1910 | 2 | – | 0.5m (1½ft) |
| | Branch brown | 889 | 869 | 2107 | – | 2 | 0.5m (1½ft) |
| | Gold | 891 | 676 | 2208 | 2 | – | 0.5m (1½ft) |
| | Ecru | 926 | Ecru | Ecru | 2 | – | 1m (1yd) |

# BUTTERFLY HAND TOWEL

Butterflies are such pretty creatures, it's hard to believe that they start out as caterpillars! There used to be many different varieties of butterfly in our gardens from early summer: perhaps it's a sign of my age, but there doesn't seem to be as many of the brightly coloured ones any more. The markings of the butterflies on this towel are all taken from real species. It just goes to show that you can't improve on Nature – only copy it!

**Design size**
18½ x 2½ (47 x 6.4cm)
**Stitch count**
257 x 37
**Materials**
Mint green hand towel, 20 x 38in (50 x 96cm)
with 14 count Aida band, 4in (10cm) wide
Threads as listed in the colour key
Size 24 tapestry needle

# WORKING THE DESIGN

Carefully measure out the centre point of the towel's Aida band, and begin stitching from here. Work the body of the large butterfly first, then the dots of detail on the wings, filling in the background colours last. Work each butterfly in this sequence, until all the cross stitch is completed, then stitch each butterfly's antennae in backstitch, in the appropriate colour.

# VARIATIONS

For a nature-friendly version of the Victorian specimen case (in which butterflies were displayed pinned to a board and mounted behind glass in a deep-rimmed frame), try stitching the butterflies in a rectangular arrangement, and frame them as a picture. Alternatively, you could stitch them randomly over a summer tablecloth to use in the garden or conservatory.

**Colour key**

| | | Anchor | DMC | Madeira | Strands for cross stitch | Strands for backstitch | Amount |
|---|---|---|---|---|---|---|---|
| | Coral | 11 | 3705 | 0213 | 2 | – | 2.5m (2yd 2ft) |
| | Dark coral | 13 | 817 | 0211 | 2 | – | 1m (1yd) |
| | Burgundy | 45 | 814 | 0514 | 2 | 1 | 3m (3yd 1ft) |
| | Dark purple | 101 | 327 | 0713 | 2 | – | 1m (1yd) |
| | Jacaranda blue | 118 | 340 | 0902 | 2 | – | 1m (1yd) |
| | Dark jacaranda blue | 119 | 333 | 0903 | 2 | – | 1m (1yd) |
| | Pale blue | 131 | 798 | 0911 | 2 | – | 2m (2yd 6in) |
| | Darkish blue | 134 | 820 | 0913 | 2 | 1 | 2m (2yd 6in) |
| | Light cornflower blue | 159 | 827 | 1710 | 2 | – | 0.5m (1½ft) |
| | Cornflower blue | 161 | 813 | 1013 | 2 | – | 0.5m (1½ft) |
| | Sandstone | 275 | 746 | 0101 | 2 | – | 1m (1yd) |
| | Autumn gold | 297 | 444 | 0108 | 2 | – | 1m (1yd) |
| | Mandarin | 324 | 721 | 0309 | 2 | – | 1.5m (1yd 2ft) |
| | Coffee brown | 351 | 400 | 2304 | 2 | 1 | 2m (2yd 6in) |
| | Ecru | 926 | Ecru | Ecru | 2 | – | 1.5m (1yd 2ft) |

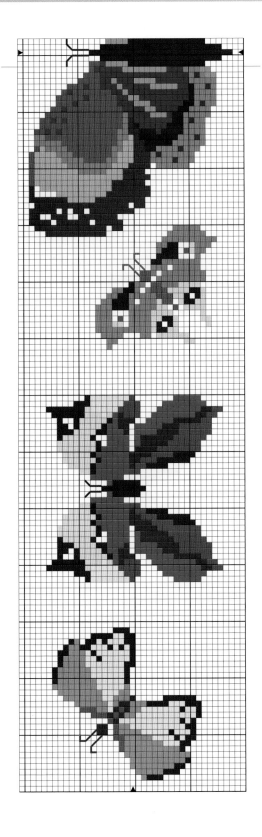

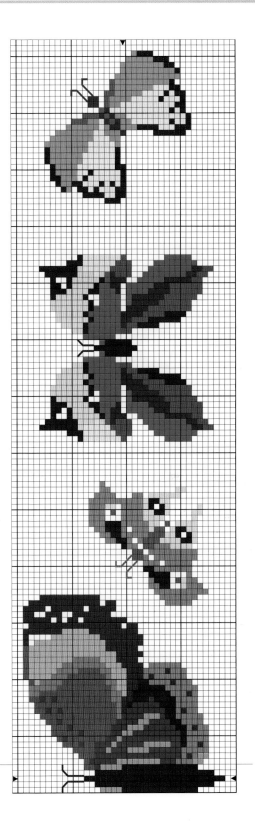

# FINISHING

**THIS CHAPTER GIVES** all the information you need to successfully finish off your needlework project. It is worth taking some time over this final stage, as a few minutes spent getting things exactly right now will make a huge difference to the presentation of the stitching you have spent hours working on.

## WASHING

Stitched fabric can be washed using either old-fashioned soap flakes or the more modern specialist needlework detergents. The detergent should be fully dispersed in lukewarm water and the fabric then immersed in this completely, and moved around gently. Do not scrub the fabric as this will damage the stitches and may distort the material. If any colours start to run (red shades are particularly unstable, although most manufacturers now state that their threads are colourfast), move the fabric quickly to plain, cold water and keep rinsing it until the dye stops running. Very carefully squeeze any excess water from the fabric, then roll it in a clean towel and squeeze it again. Do not wring the fabric – again this may cause damage and distortion. Unroll the towel and remove the fabric, placing it somewhere flat and clean, like an ironing board, to dry thoroughly.

## PRESSING

To press your work, first pad your ironing board with a couple of thick towels, then place the stitching face down on top of them. You can place a slightly damp handkerchief on top to protect it even further, but this isn't essential. Use a steam iron on a medium setting and do not press too hard or your stitches may become flattened: the steam should do most of the work for you.

## BLOCKING

When your stitching is complete, especially if you have not used a frame, you may need to block it to get it square. To do this, place the fabric face down on a board generously covered with blotting paper or sheeting (see Fig 12). Dampen the fabric with water

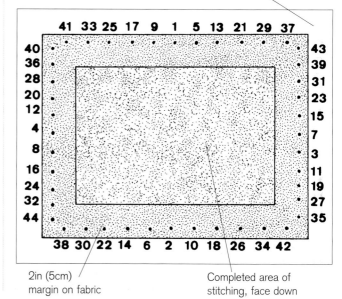

**Fig 12. Blocking the fabric – pinning order.**

Fibreboard covered with blotting paper

2in (5cm) margin on fabric

Completed area of stitching, face down

from a houseplant sprayer. Then, using drawing pins at ½in (1cm) intervals, pin it out evenly, starting at the mid-point of each side, and gradually working towards each corner, pulling the fabric square as you go. Leave it to dry completely.

## MOUNTING AND FRAMING

If you want to use wadding under your fabric to raise it slightly, cut a piece of 2oz wadding to the size of your mount board (if you are using a coloured mount in the frame as well, cut the wadding to the size of the aperture). Centre your stitching on the mount board, and push dressmaker's pins through the fabric and into the top edge of the board, using the holes in the fabric to ensure that you are pinning it straight (see Fig 13). Gently pull the fabric taut, and repeat the process along the bottom edge, and the two sides. Using a long piece of strong thread, such as crochet cotton, lace the fabric from side to side across the back, working stitches every inch (2.5cm) or so. Pull up the slack before tying off securely. Repeat for the top and bottom edges. Fold in the corners and slip stitch down, if necessary (see Fig 14). Remove the pins.

**Fig 13. Pinning fabric onto mount board.**

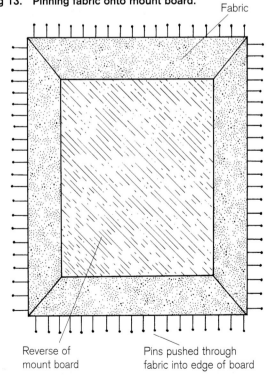

Fabric

Reverse of mount board

Pins pushed through fabric into edge of board

**Fig 14. Lacing fabric to mount board.**

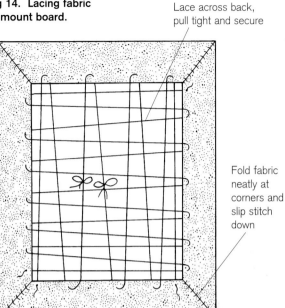

Lace across back, pull tight and secure

Fold fabric neatly at corners and slip stitch down

Your stitching is now ready to be placed in the frame, either with or without glass.

## HEMMING

Such items as tablecloths, traycloths, and placemats can all be neatened by hemming. Simply trim the fabric to the size you want, plus 1in (2.5cm) all round. Turn the fabric under and under again, and slip stitch in place (see Fig 15). Alternatively, you can use a sewing machine to stitch the hem down, using a thread to match the fabric colour. You only need to turn Aida under once, if using a sewing machine, as it is quite thick fabric. Evenweave needs to be turned under twice, as it is quite 'springy', and frays easily.

**Fig 15. Hemming an edge.**

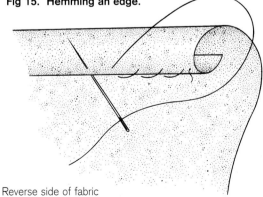

Reverse side of fabric

# CURTAIN
# TIE-BACK
# TEMPLATE

To get a full template, trace outline onto a folded sheet of paper, cut around tracing, then open out.

**Fig 16. Template for curtain tie-backs.**

Place fold here

# METRIC CONVERSION TABLE

**inches to millimetres and centimetres**

| in | mm | cm | in | cm | in | cm |
|----|----|----|----|----|----|----|
| ⅛ | 3 | 0.3 | 9 | 22.9 | 30 | 76.2 |
| ¼ | 6 | 0.6 | 10 | 25.4 | 31 | 78.7 |
| ⅜ | 10 | 1.0 | 11 | 27.9 | 32 | 81.3 |
| ½ | 13 | 1.3 | 12 | 30.5 | 33 | 83.8 |
| ⅝ | 16 | 1.6 | 13 | 33.0 | 34 | 86.4 |
| ¾ | 19 | 1.9 | 14 | 35.6 | 35 | 88.9 |
| ⅞ | 22 | 2.2 | 15 | 38.1 | 36 | 91.4 |
| 1 | 25 | 2.5 | 16 | 40.6 | 37 | 94.0 |
| 1¼ | 32 | 3.2 | 17 | 43.2 | 38 | 96.5 |
| 1½ | 38 | 3.8 | 18 | 45.7 | 39 | 99.1 |
| 1¾ | 44 | 4.4 | 19 | 48.3 | 40 | 101.6 |
| 2 | 51 | 5.1 | 20 | 50.8 | 41 | 104.1 |
| 2½ | 64 | 6.4 | 21 | 53.3 | 42 | 106.7 |
| 3 | 76 | 7.6 | 22 | 55.9 | 43 | 109.2 |
| 3½ | 89 | 8.9 | 23 | 58.4 | 44 | 111.8 |
| 4 | 102 | 10.2 | 24 | 61.0 | 45 | 114.3 |
| 4½ | 114 | 11.4 | 25 | 63.5 | 46 | 116.8 |
| 5 | 127 | 12.7 | 26 | 66.0 | 47 | 119.4 |
| 6 | 152 | 15.2 | 27 | 68.6 | 48 | 121.9 |
| 7 | 178 | 17.8 | 28 | 71.1 | 49 | 124.5 |
| 8 | 203 | 20.3 | 29 | 73.7 | 50 | 127.0 |

# SUPPLIERS

All of these companies provide a mail-order service. Most of them have a catalogue, for which there may be a charge. Please telephone (or write, enclosing an SAE) to find out the cost of any catalogue.

## UNITED KINGDOM

### Cotswold Needlecraft Centre
11 The Huntings
Church Close
Broadway
Worcestershire WR12 7AH
Tel/Fax: 01386 858050

Full range of fabrics, threads, etc.

### Craft Creations Ltd
Units 1–7
Harpers Yard
Ruskin Rd
Tottenham
London
N17 8QA
Tel: 0181 885 2655
Fax: 0181 808 0746

Card mounts (e.g. bookmarks etc.) for mounting all types of craft work.

### Framecraft Miniatures Ltd
372–376 Summer Lane
Hockley
Birmingham
B19 3QA
Tel: 0121 212 0551
Fax: 0121 212 0552

Acrylic products, such as coasters and fingerplates. Also wooden frames and mounts for needlework.

### Willow Fabrics
27 Willow Green
Knutsford
Cheshire
WA16 6AX
Tel: 01565 621 098

Full range of fabrics, threads etc.

### Wimble Bees
Unit 4
Manor Farm Barns
Wantage
Oxfordshire
OX12 8NE
Tel/Fax: 01235 771731

Mail order only. Stock a large range of fabrics, threads, mounts, accessories etc., for all types of needlework.

## UNITED STATES

### Anne Brinkley Designs Inc.
761 Palmer Ave
Holmdel
NJ 977333
Tel: (0908) 787 2100

United States distributor for Framecraft products.

### Gay Bowles Sales Inc.
P.O. Box 1060
Janesville
WI 53547
Tel: (0608) 754 9466

United States distributor for Framecraft products.

## AUSTRALIA

### Stadia Handicrafts
85 Elizabeth St
Paddington
NSW
2021
Tel: (02) 328 7973
Fax: (02) 326 1768

Fabrics, threads etc.

### Ireland Needlecraft Pty Ltd
4, 2–4 Keppel Dr
Hallam
Vic
3803
Tel: (03) 702 3222

Australian distributor for Framecraft products.

## NEW ZEALAND

### The Embroidery Shop
286 Queen St
Masterton
Tel: (06) 377 1418

New Zealand distributor for Framecraft products.

### Nancy's Embroidery Ltd
326 Tinakori Rd
Thorndon
Wellington
Tel: (04) 473 4047

## CANADA

### Danish Art Needlework
P.O. Box 442
Lethbridge
Alberta
T1J 3Z1
Tel: (0403) 327 9855

Canadian distributor for Framecraft products.

# INDEX

# ABOUT THE AUTHOR

**JANET GRANGER** was born in Hornchurch, Essex. She has had an interest in embroidery since the age of 12, creating her first designs at the age of 14, and had two exhibitions of her needlework while still in her teens.

After leaving school at 16, she worked in public libraries for 17 years, before deciding to concentrate on building up a business designing and marketing her own range of miniature needlepoint carpet kits for collectors' dolls' houses. In November 1996, she reached the finals of the British Miniaturist of the Year competition with four of her carpet designs. Her first book, *Miniature Needlepoint Carpets*, also published by Guild of Master Craftsman Publications, features 25 designs from this range.

In the small amount of free time that she has, Janet is studying with the Open University towards a Social Science degree.

## BOOKS

# WOODWORKING

| | | | |
|---|---|---|---|
| 40 More Woodworking Plans & Projects | GMC Publications | Making Shaker Furniture | Barry Jackson |
| Bird Boxes and Feeders for the Garden | Dave Mackenzie | Making Tables and Chairs | GMC Publications |
| Complete Woodfinishing | Ian Hosker | Making Unusual Miniatures | Graham Spalding |
| Electric Woodwork | Jeremy Broun | Pine Furniture Projects | Dave Mackenzie |
| Furniture Projects | Rod Wales | Security for the Householder: | |
| Furniture Restoration (Practical Crafts) | Kevin Jan Bonner | Lock Fitting and other Devices | E. Phillips |
| Furniture Restoration For Beginners | Kevin Jan Bonner | Sharpening Pocket Reference Book | Jim Kingshott |
| Green Woodwork | Barry Jackson | Sharpening: The Complete Guide | Jim Kingshott |
| Incredible Router | Jeremy Broun | The Workshop | Jim Kingshott |
| Making & Modifying Woodworking Tools | Jim Kingshott | Tool Making for Woodworkers | Ray Larsen |
| Making Fine Furniture | Tom Darby | Woodfinishing Handbook (Practical Crafts) | Ian Hosker |
| Making Little Boxes from Wood | John Bennett | Woodworking Plans & Projects | GMC Publications |

# WOODTURNING

| | | | |
|---|---|---|---|
| Adventures in Woodturning | David Springett | Practical Tips for Woodturners | GMC Publications |
| Bert Marsh: Woodturner | Bert Marsh | Practical Tips for Woodturners – Book 2 | GMC Publications |
| Bill Jones' Further Notes from the Turning Shop | Bill Jones | Spindle Turning | GMC Publications |
| Bill Jones' Notes from the Turning Shop | Bill Jones | Turning Miniatures in Wood | John Sainsbury |
| Colouring Techniques for Woodturners | Jan Sanders | Turning Wooden Toys | Terry Lawrence |
| Decorative Techniques For Woodturners | Hilary Bowen | Understanding Woodturning | Ann & Bob Phillips |
| Faceplate Turning | GMC Publications | Useful Woodturning Projects | GMC Publications |
| Fun at the Lathe | R.C.Bell | Woodturning Jewellery | Hilary Bowen |
| Illustrated Woodturning Techniques | John Hunnex | Woodturning Masterclass | Tony Boase |
| Keith Rowley's Woodturning Projects | Keith Rowley | Woodturning Projects | GMC Publications |
| Make Money from Woodturning | Ann & Bob Phillips | Woodturning Techniques | GMC Publications |
| Multi-Centre Woodturning | Ray Hopper | Woodturning Wizardry | David Springett |
| Pleasure and Profit from Woodturning | Reg Sherwin | Woodturning: A Foundation Course | Keith Rowley |
| Practical Tips for Turners & Carvers | GMC Publications | Woodturning: A Sourcebook of Shapes | John Hunnex |

# WOODCARVING

| | | | |
|---|---|---|---|
| Carving Birds & Beasts | GMC Publications | The Woodcarvers | GMC Publications |
| Carving on Turning | GMC Publications | Understanding Woodcarving | GMC Publications |
| Carving Realistic Birds | David Tippey | Wildfowl Carving – Volume 1 | Jim Pearce |
| Decorative Woodcarving | Jeremy Williams | Wildfowl Carving – Volume 2 | Jim Pearce |
| Essential Woodcarving Techniques | Dick Onians | Woodcarving for Beginners | GMC Publications |
| Lettercarving in Wood | Chris Pye | Woodcarving Tools, Materials & Equipment | Chris Pye |
| Practical Tips for Woodcarvers – Book 2 | GMC Publications | Woodcarving: A Complete Course | Ron Butterfield |
| The Art of the Woodcarver | GMC Publications | Woodcarving: A Foundation Course | Zoë Gertner |

# UPHOLSTERY

| | | | |
|---|---|---|---|
| Seat Weaving (Practical Crafts) | Ricky Holdstock | Upholstery Techniques & Projects | David James |
| Upholsterer's Pocket Reference Book | David James | Upholstery: A Complete Course | David James |
| Upholstery Restoration Projects | David James | | |

# TOYMAKING

| | | | |
|---|---|---|---|
| Designing & Making Wooden Toys | Terry Kelly | Making Wooden Toys & Games | Jeff & Jennie Loader |
| Fun to Make Wooden Toys and Games | Jeff & Jennie Loader | Restoring Rocking Horses | Clive Green & Anthony Dew |
| Making Board Peg & Dice Games | Jeff & Jennie Loader | | |

# DOLLS' HOUSES

| | | | |
|---|---|---|---|
| Architecture for Dolls' Houses | Joyce Percival | Making Period Dolls' House Accessories | Andrea Barham |
| Beginners' Guide to the Dolls' House Hobby | Jean Nisbett | Making Period Dolls' House Furniture | Derek & Sheila Rowbottom |
| Dolls' House Bathrooms – Lots of Little Loos | Patricia King | Making Tudor Dolls' Houses | Derek & Sheila Rowbottom |
| Easy to Make Dolls' House Accessories | Andrea Barham | Making Victorian Dolls' House Furniture | Patricia King |
| Make Your Own Dolls' House Furniture | Maurice Harper | Miniature Needlepoint Carpets | Janet Granger |
| Making Dolls' House Furniture | Patricia King | The Secrets of the Dolls' House Makers | Jean Nisbett |
| Making Georgian Dolls' Houses | Derek & Sheila Rowbottom | The Complete Dolls' House Book | Jean Nisbett |

# CRAFTS

| | | | |
|---|---|---|---|
| Celtic Knotwork Designs | Sheila Sturrock | Embroidery Tips & Hints | Harold Hayes |
| Collage from Seeds, Leaves and Flowers | Joan Carver | Introduction to Pyrography (Practical Crafts) | Stephen Poole |
| Complete Pyrography | Stephen Poole | Making Knitwear Fit | Pat Ashforth & Steve Plummer |
| Creating Knitwear Designs | Pat Ashforth & Steve Plummer | Tassel Making for Beginners | Enid Taylor |
| Cross Stitch Kitchen Projects | Janet Granger | Tatting Collage | Lindsay Rogers |
| Cross Stitch on Colour | Sheena Rogers | | |

# VIDEOS

| | | | |
|---|---|---|---|
| Drop-in and Pinstuffed Seats | David James | Classic Profiles | Dennis White |
| Stuffover Upholstery | David James | Twists and Advanced Turning | Dennis White |
| Elliptical Turning | David Springett | Sharpening The Professional Way | Jim Kingshott |
| Woodturning Wizardry | David Springett | Sharpening Turning & Carving Tools | Jim Kingshott |
| Turning Between Centres | Dennis White | Bowl Turning | John Jordan |
| Turning Bowls | Dennis White | Hollow Turning | John Jordan |
| Boxes, Goblets & Screw Threads | Dennis White | Woodturning: A Foundation Course | Keith Rowley |
| Novelties and Projects | Dennis White | Carving A Figure – The Female Form | Ray Gonzales |

# MAGAZINES

## WOODTURNING • WOODCARVING • TOYMAKING
## FURNITURE & CABINETMAKING • BUSINESSMATTERS
## CREATIVE IDEAS FOR THE HOME • THE ROUTER

The above represents a full list of all titles currently published or scheduled to be published. All are available direct from the Publishers or through bookshops, newsagents and specialist retailers. To place an order, or to obtain a complete catalogue, contact:

GMC PUBLICATIONS, 166 HIGH STREET, LEWES, EAST SUSSEX BN7 1XU UNITED KINGDOM
TEL: 01273 488005 FAX: 01273 478606

ORDERS BY CREDIT CARD ARE ACCEPTED